Stay Fit & Healthy
UNTIL YOU'RE DEAD

Stay Fit & Healthy
UNTIL YOU'RE DEAD

By Dave Barry

**ILLUSTRATED BY
JERRY O'BRIEN**

Rodale Press, Emmaus, Pennsylvania

Printed in the United States of America on
recycled paper containing a high percentage of
deinked fiber.

Book design by Anita G. Patterson

**Library of Congress Cataloging in
Publication Data**

Barry, Dave.
    Stay fit and healthy until you're dead.

    Includes index.
    1. Health—Anecdotes, facetiae, satire, etc.
I. Title.
PN6231.H38B37   1985   613'.0207
    85-11931
ISBN 0-87857-570-7   paperback

2 4 6 8 10 9 7 5 3   paperback

Contents

Inspirational Opening Anecdote Explaining the Author's Lifelong Personal Commitment to Health and Fitness

Thirty-one years ago, when I was a mere boy of seven, my mother fell very, very sick. She called me to her side and, in a voice weakened by pain, said, "Bob, whatever happens to me, I want you to remember that . . ."

"David," I corrected. "My name is David."

"I know that, you little snot," she said. "I'm your mother."

I have always remembered those words, despite the fact that my mother recovered completely and is fine today.

Hi, Mom.

Introduction

Four Reasons Why You Must Get Fit Immediately

1. YOU OWE IT TO YOUR COUNTRY. You can bet that the enemies of your country are fit. People in Communist nations are on a strict fitness program of waiting in line a lot and darting their eyes about nervously. We, too, must be fit, in case these Communists invade us. We must be ready to fight them in the streets and the alleys. The problem is that many of you have eaten so many Enormous Economy Size bags of corn chips and so much bean

dip that you probably couldn't fit into the alleys without the aid of powerful hydraulic devices. So you'd have to fight them in the streets, where you'd be easy prey for their blimp-seeking missiles.

2. YOU OWE IT TO YOUR CAREER. In the old days, your successful business executive was generally a spectacular tub of lard who had to be transported from business deal to business deal via private railroad car. But today's top executives are lean, sleek, and fit. They eat nutritionally balanced meals, run ten miles every day, play tennis and racquetball, and work out regularly on Nautilus machines. Consequently, they have no time whatsoever for their work. Many of them don't even know where their offices are. This is why the entire U.S. economy is now manufactured in Japan.

3. YOU OWE IT TO YOUR SELF-ESTEEM. There is no feeling in the world quite as wonderful as the feeling of being physically fit, except the feeling of eating pepperoni pizza. No! Wait! Disregard that last remark! What I'm trying to say is, when you become fit, everything about you changes. You have to buy new pants, for example. And you develop a whole new attitude about yourself. Instead of constantly thinking, "I am pasty and flabby and disgusting and nobody likes me," you think, "People like me now, but only as long as I can keep from becoming pasty and flabby and disgusting again. I wish I had a pepperoni pizza."

4. YOU OWE IT TO YOUR FUTURE. There's nothing like regular, vigorous exercise to prepare you for the pain you'll inevitably have to endure when you get older. Let's say you're in your mid-20s to mid-30s. Most of the time you feel pretty good, right? The only time you feel lousy is when you ingest huge quantities of alcohol and wake up the next day in an unfamiliar city naked with unexplained chest wounds. But as you grow older, you're going to start feeling more aches and pains caused by the inevitable afflictions of age, such as the Social Security Administration, condescending denture adhesive commercials, and your children.

People who exercise regularly are prepared for this pain. Take joggers: you see them plodding along, clearly hating every minute of it, and you think, "What's the point?" But years from now, when you're struggling to adjust to the pains of the aging process, the joggers, who have been in constant agony for 20 years, will be able to make

the transition smoothly, unless they're already dead (see Chapter 12, under "Fitness and the Afterlife").

How Insects Stay Fit

We can learn a great deal about fitness from observing insects. You have probably noticed, for example, that most ants are in excellent shape. You almost never see a fat ant. What makes this especially interesting is that ants are always lugging around disgusting junk food, such as discarded Cracker Jacks many times the ants' own size.

So how do ants stay so fit? The answer is surprisingly simple: they have no mouths.

And this is a good thing, really, because it means they can't scream when you spray them with Raid, although they do their best to writhe around in a piteous manner.

So anyway, what we have, in the ant, is a creature that engages in strenuous physical exercise all day long and never eats any-thing. This is Nature's Way to fitness, and we should emulate it if we wish to have the kind of taut, firm bodies that make ants the envy of the insect kingdom. Of course, we must always weigh this against the fact that they have a life span of maybe six weeks and are subject to attack by vicious beetles.

TRUE TESTIMONY FROM AMERICA'S LEADING PHYSICAL FITNESS BUFFS...

ARNOLD SCHWARZENEGGER BEFORE READING THIS BOOK: "IT READ REAL GOOD"

JANE FONDA BEFORE READING THIS BOOK: "DAVE WHO?"

MR.T BEFORE READING THIS BOOK: "IT'S BAD, REAL BAD"

TRIGGER BEFORE CHEWING ON THIS BOOK: "NAY"

WOODY ALLEN BEFORE READING THIS BOOK: "PLAY IT AGAIN, DAVE"

DOLLY PARTON BEFORE READING THIS BOOK: "LEARNED ME REAL GOOD"

So the Bottom Line Is . . .

. . . now is the time to start that fitness program! Fitness is more than just another new "craze," like flavored popcorn or parenthood. Fitness is a philosophy of life, a revolutionary new concept in personhood, and, ultimately, a way for people like me to become wealthy via the sales of fitness-related items such as this book.

But people like me can do only so much. We can take your money. After that, it's up to you. If you don't follow the diet and exercise program outlined in this book, it won't do you a bit of good. Even if you do follow it, it may not do you any good. Nobody really knows what will happen. You'll be the first person who ever actually tried this particular program. I meant to try it myself, before the book got published, but I had to buy snow tires. So maybe it would be a good idea to have a friend try it first, as a sort of test, and watch to see whether he actually does become fit, or starts lapsing into lengthy comas or something.

Well, that's enough of a pep talk. Let's square our shoulders and take that first step toward Becoming a Fitter You. Those of you who are unable to simultaneously square your shoulders and take a step may do them one at a time.

How Fit Are You?

The first step in your new fitness program is to take the three simple tests below so we can find out how fit you are right now. Be sure to write down the results as you go along, so the police will be able to figure out what happened.

1. BODY FAT TEST

You'll need:

A swimming pool

A dozen concrete blocks

Some stout rope

A knife

A primitive denizen of some remote fungal island in the South Pacific

Directions: Fat tends to make you float, so the idea here is to determine how many concrete blocks have to be lashed to your body to make you stay on the bottom of the pool for at least a minute without bobbing to the surface. Have your denizen perch by the side of the pool with the knife clenched in his teeth so he can dive down to cut you loose after the minute elapses.

(Caution: Some of your more primitive denizens have no understanding whatsoever of time, so their concept of a minute may in fact be closer to what we in Western Civilization think of us a fortnight. Also, whatever you do, don't give your denizen one of those Swiss army knives with all the various confusing attachments. You don't want him swimming down there and sawing at your rope with the spoon.)

How to score: Count the number of blocks required to keep you submerged. More than eight is very bad.

2. HEART TEST
You'll need:
A friend
A job at an office building with elevators
A scorpion

Directions: Give the scorpion to your friend, and instruct him or her to wait a couple of weeks, until you've completely forgotten about it, then sneak up behind you at work and hurl it into the elevator with you just as the doors close. What we're looking to determine here is whether your heart is strong enough to handle the rigors of an exercise program.

How to score: Give yourself a 5 if your heart continues to beat unassisted. If

you score any lower than that, you probably shouldn't do this particular test.

3. AEROBICS TEST
You'll need:
A stopwatch
Gerald Ford

Directions: The word "aerobics" comes from two Greek words: _aero,_ meaning "ability to," and _bics,_ meaning "withstand tremendous boredom." This is the difference between a world-class marathon runner and a normal person: a world-class marathon runner has undergone sufficient aerobic conditioning that he can run for nearly three hours without falling asleep, whereas a normal person will quit after a few minutes and look for something interesting to do.

What you want to do in this test is start your stopwatch, then see how long you can listen to Gerald Ford discuss the federal deficit before you doze off. If Gerald Ford is unavailable, you can use televised golf.

How to score: 15 seconds is excellent. More than 30 seconds indicates some kind of brain damage.

CALCULATING YOUR FINAL "FITNESS QUOTIENT"

Divide your age by the number of blocks it took to hold you on the bottom of the pool, then add the number of seconds it took for Gerald Ford to sedate you multiplied by your scorpion score, unless you are claiming two or more exemptions. This will give you your "fitness quotient"; store it wherever you keep the instructions for operating your various digital watches.

Important Medical Note

Before you begin any fitness program, you should, of course, have your doctor give you a thorough physical examination in which he shoves cold steel implements into your various bodily orifices and sticks needles directly into your skin and makes you put on a flimsy garment apparently made from a cocktail napkin and parade through the waiting room carrying a transparent container filled with your own urine past several people you hope to someday ask for jobs. Or, if you'd prefer not to undergo this procedure, you may simply send your doctor some money.

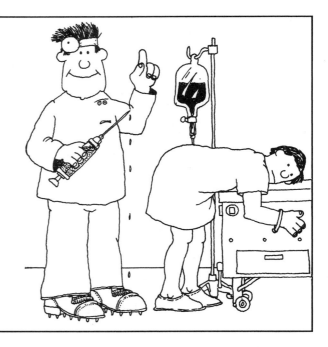

Chapter 1

How Your Body Works

Your body is like a superbly engineered luxury automobile: if you use it wisely and maintain it properly, it will eventually break down, most likely in a bad neighborhood. To understand why this is, let's take a look inside this fascinating "machine" we call the human body.

Your body is actually made up of billions and billions of tiny cells, called "cells," which are so small that you cannot see them. Neither can I. The only people who can see them are white-coated geeks called "biologists." These are the people who wrote your high-school biology textbooks, in which they claimed to have found all these organs inside the Frog, the Worm, and the Perch. Remember? And remember how, in Biology Lab, you were supposed to take an actual dead frog apart and locate the heart, the liver, etc., as depicted in the elaborate color diagrams in the textbook?

Of course, when you cut it open, all you ever found was frog glop, because that is what frogs contain, as has been proven in countless experiments performed by small boys with sticks. So you did what biology students have always done: you pretended you were finding all these organs in there,

and you copied the diagram out of the book, knowing full well that in real life a frog would have no use whatsoever for a liver.

Anyway, biologists tell us that the human body consists of billions of these tiny cells, which combine to form organs such as the heart, the kidney, the eyeball, the funny bone, the clavichord, the pustule, and the hernia, which in turn combine to form the body, which in turn combines with other bodies to form the squadron. Now let's take

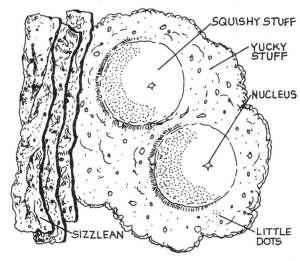

SQUISHY STUFF
YUCKY STUFF
NUCLEUS
SIZZLEAN
LITTLE DOTS

a closer look at the various fitness-related organs and see if we can't think of things to say about them.

The Skin

Your skin performs several vital functions. For example, it keeps people from

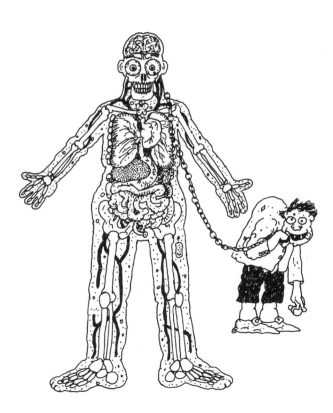

seeing the inside of your body, which is repulsive, and it prevents your organs from falling out onto the ground, where careless pedestrians might step on them. Also, without skin, your body would have no place to form large facial zits on the morning before your wedding.

But for fitness-oriented persons like yourself, the important thing about skin is that it acts as your Body's Cooling System. Whenever you exercise or get on an elevator, sweat oozes out of millions of tiny skin holes so it can evaporate and cool the area. Unfortunately, virtually all of these holes are located in your armpits, which is stupid. I mean, you hardly ever hear people complaining about having hot armpits. So what we seem to have here is one of those cases where Mother Nature really screwed up, like when she developed the concept of nasal hair.

The Muscle System

Your muscles are what enable you to perform all of your basic movements, such as bowling, sniping, pandering, carping, and contacting your attorney. Basically, there are two kinds of muscle tissue: the kind that people in advertisements for fitness centers have, which forms units that look like sleek and powerful pythons writhing just beneath the surface of the skin, and the kind you

FITNESS AD MUSCLES   YOUR MUSCLES

have, which looks more like deceased baby rabbits.

The beauty of muscle tissue, however, is that it responds to exercise. In a later chapter, we'll talk about how, using modern exercise equipment such as the Nautilus machine in a scientific workout program, you can stretch those pudgy little muscle tissues of yours to the point where you won't even be able to scream for help without the aid of powerful painkilling drugs.

The Skeletal System

How many bones do you think your skeletal system has? Would you say 50? 150? 250? 300? More than 300?

If you guessed 50, you're a real jerk. I would say it's around 250, but I don't really see why it's all that important. The only important part of your skeleton, for fitness purposes, is your knees.

Knees are God's way of telling mankind that He doesn't want us to do anything really strenuous. When we do, our knees punish us by becoming injured, as you know if you've ever watched professional football on television:

ANNOUNCER: The handoff goes to Burger; he's tackled at the six. . . . Uh oh! He's hurt!
COLOR COMMENTATOR: Looks like a knee injury, Bob, from the way that bone there is sticking out of his knee.
ANNOUNCER: Burger's teammates are bending over him. . . . Uh oh! Now *they're* down on the field!
COLOR COMMENTATOR: Looks like they've all injured their knees, too, Bob.
ANNOUNCER: Here comes the team physician, who is. . . . Uh oh! Now *he's* down on the. . . .

So one of the things we're going to stress in our fitness program is knee safety. We're going to get you so aware of this important topic that you won't even discuss racquetball over the telephone without first putting on knee braces the size of industrial turbines.

The Digestive System

Your digestive system is your body's Fun House, whereby food goes on a long, dark, scary ride, taking all kinds of unexpected twists and turns, being attacked by vicious secretions along the way, and not knowing until the last minute whether it will be turned into a useful body part or ejected into the Dark Hole by Mister Sphincter. You must be careful about what you eat, unless you want your body making heart valves out of things like bean dip.

The Central Nervous System

The central nervous system is your body's Messenger, always letting your brain know what's going on elsewhere in your body. "Your nose itches!" it tells your brain. Or, "Your foot is falling asleep!!" Or, "You're hungry!!!" All day long, your brain hears messages like these, thousands of them, hour after hour, until finally it deliberately rests your hand on a red-hot stove just for the pleasure of hearing your nervous system scream in pain.

Your Respiratory System

Your respiratory system takes in oxygen and gives off carbon monoxide, a deadly gas, by a process called "photosynthesis." This takes place in your lungs, yam-shaped organs in your chest containing millions of tiny little air sacs, called "Bernice." In a normal person, these sacs are healthy and pink, whereas in smokers they have the wretched, soot-stained, anguished look of the people fleeing Atlanta in *Gone with the Wind*. This has led many noted medical researchers to conclude that smoking is unhealthy, but we must weigh this against the fact that most of the people in cigarette advertisements are generally horse-riding, helicopter-flying hunks of major-league manhood, whereas your noted medical researchers tend to be pasty little wimps of the variety that you routinely held upside down over the toilet in junior high school.

The Circulatory System

This is, of course, your heart, a fist-sized muscle in your chest with a two-inch-thick layer of greasy fat clinging to it consisting of every Milky Way you ever ate. Your heart's job is to pump your blood, which appears to be nothing more than a red liquid but which, according to biologists (this should come as no surprise), is actually teeming with millions of organisms, some of them with tentacles so they can teem more efficiently.

The only organisms that actually belong in your blood are the red cells and the white cells. The red cells are your body's Room Service, carrying tiny particles of food and oxygen to the other organs, which snork them up without so much as a "thank you." The only reward the red cells get is iron in the form of prunes, which the other cells don't want anyway. If you don't eat enough prunes, your red cells get tired—a condition doctors call "tired blood"—and you have to lie down and watch "All My Children."

The white cells are your body's House Detectives. Most of the time they lounge around the bloodstream, telling jokes and forming the occasional cyst. But they swing into action the instant your body is invaded by one of the many enemy organisms that can get into your bloodstream, these being bacteria, viruses, rotifers, conifers, parameciums, cholesterol, tiny little lockjaw germs that dwell on the ends of all sharp objects, antacids, riboflavin, and the plague. As soon as the white cells spot one of these, they drop whatever they're doing and pursue it on a wild and often hilarious chase through your various organs, which sometimes results in damage to innocent tissue. Eventually they catch the invader and tie its tentacles behind its back with antibodies, which are the body's Handcuffs, and deport it via the bowel.

Of course this is just a brief rundown on your various organs and systems; in the short space I have here, it's very difficult for me to explain all of your body's complexities and subtleties in any detail, or even get any facts right. For more information, I suggest you attend Harvard Medical School, which I believe is in Wisconsin.

Meanwhile, let's turn the page and really get started on our fitness program! Or at least limber up.

Chapter 2

Getting Ready to Get Started

One of the most exciting aspects of getting into fitness is that you get to wear modern fitness-oriented clothing, clothing that makes a statement to the world around you. "Look," it states, "I have purchased some fitness-oriented clothing."

Up until about 15 years ago, the only fitness clothing available for men was the plain grey sweat suit, which we fitness experts now recognize as totally inadequate in terms of retail markup. Fitness wear for females consisted of those high-school gym outfits colored Digestive Enzyme Green; there was no fitness clothing available at all for adult women, because the only forms of exercise deemed appropriate for them were labor and driving station wagons.

As the fitness craze developed, however, all kinds of "active sportswear" became available from famous designers who think

STANDARD 1965 (OR SO) MALE GYM SUITS

STANDARD 1965 (OR SO) FEMALE GYM SUITS

nothing of putting their names on your clothing, but who would have the servants set the dogs on you if you ever tried to put your name on *their* clothing. Today it's not uncommon for people to wear their active sportswear to the shopping mall, to work, to the opera, to state funerals, etc. Recently, an attorney argued a major case before the U.S. Supreme Court while wearing a puce jogging outfit! The justices didn't seem to mind at all, although this could also have been partly because they had fallen asleep.

The point is, you want to choose your fitness-program clothing carefully because chances are you'll be wearing it to do much more than just exercise. In fact, you'll probably be wearing it to do everything *but* exercise, since there is growing medical evidence that exercise can make you tired and sweaty, as we'll see in later chapters.

The Basic Fitness Fashion Look for Women

This is, of course, the leotard and tights, which is the preferred outfit because it shows every bodily flaw a woman has, no matter how minute, so that a woman who, disguised in her street clothes, looks like Victoria Principal will, when she puts on her leotard, transform herself into Bertha the

Choosing the Correct Leotard Size

The correct leotard size for you depends, of course, on your body type. Use this handy chart as a guide:

BODY TYPE   LEOTARD SIZE

•

•

•

Amazing Land Whale. This encourages her to exercise vigorously and watch what she eats. She cannot, of course, drink anything, as there is no way to go to the bathroom in a leotard and tights.

Many a woman who suffers an exercise-related injury during an aerobic workout is forced to lie in great pain for hours on her exercise mat, trapped, while frustrated rescue personnel wait for the helicopter to bring the various specialized torches, saws, and other equipment they need to free her from her tights and leotard so they can render medical treatment.

Extremely Important Advice Concerning Danskin Brand Thermal Calf Protection Devices

Several years ago, a crack team of medical fashion experts determined that cold air tends to form pockets around the calves of fashionable, fitness-oriented women (see illustration). This breakthrough discovery explained the sudden upsurge in calf-related hospitalizations that occurred at the onset of the fitness craze and soon reached epidemic proportions. As one nationally reknowned physician, whose name is available upon request, put it, "Never in my 600 years of practicing medicine had I seen so

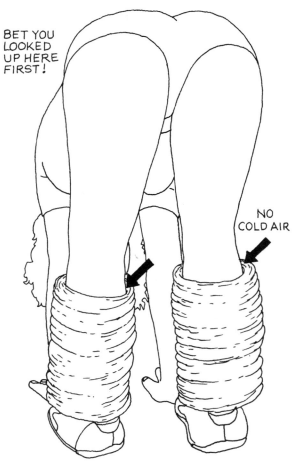

CALF PROTECTION DEVICES

many deaths directly attributable to calf coldness. If only we had known then the importance of wearing Danskin brand thermal calf protection devices!"

So the bottom line is: Do not view these devices as just another semiretarded fashion trend. View them as essential medical protection, every bit as important as lip gloss.

Fitness Fashion for Men

What you want, men, is a fashion look that gives you freedom of movement but at the same time displays, in large letters, the names of at least three major manufacturers of sporting equipment. Also you want to wear a headband and wristbands to absorb the tremendous outpouring of sweat that we males emit when we are engaged in strenuous masculine physical activity. (If you are one of those unfortunate males who does not emit tremendous outpourings of sweat, you should purchase, from the Nike Corporation, a container of "Pro-spiration" spray-on sweat droplets, which you apply discreetly in the locker room before you begin your workout.)

Ideally, of course, you will also sport some evidence of a semicrippling football injury. The best kind is a medical knee contraption of such enormous size and complexity that your racquetball opponent will feel like absolute pond scum if he hits the ball anywhere other than directly to you. Or you might want to look into a new product from the Adidas Corporation called "The All-

Scars," which are large, realistic, and extremely repulsive synthetic removable knee scars patterned after those belonging to famous battered sports legends such as Joe Namath.

Fitness with Computers

Can you use a personal home computer in your fitness program? You bet! Computers are incredibly versatile machines that can do everything from screw up your airplane reservation to cause an income tax blunder that gets you sentenced to a life term in a slimy walled federal prison so utterly desolate that the inmates pay rodents for sex! So they're a "natural" for the fitness movement!

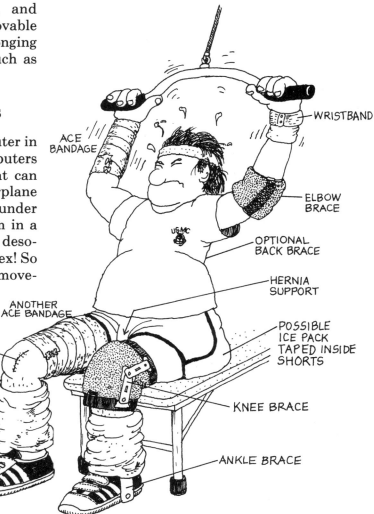

TYPICAL FAKE INJURY EQUIPMENT

One obvious way to use a computer, of course, is to record your daily fitness statistics such as weight, height, age, etc., on it, using a felt-tipped marker (see illustration). But the best way to really unleash the power of a computer is to lift it up and set it down repeatedly, thus building muscle mass and definition. As you become stronger, you can gradually add weight, in the form of "disk drives," until eventually you move up to a heavier computer—and perhaps someday even reach the point where you can hoist what computer bodybuilding enthusiasts call a "mainframe" computer!

For the average person who does not have a background in data processing, I generally

DON'T OVERLOOK THE COMPUTER'S PACKING BOX
AS A SURFACE TO ENTER YOUR STATISTICS

recommend starting out with a 35-pound computer. Unfortunately, computer weights are measured not in pounds, but in "K's" (as in 512K), which stands for "kilograms." There is a way to convert kilograms to pounds, but it is almost always fatal, so I recommend, as a wise consumer tip, that you go through your entire planned computer-lifting routine right at the store with several reputable computers, checking each for heft, balance, and tendency to break into 600,000 tiny pieces when you lift it over your head and drop it, before you actually purchase anything.

Of course, some of you, and here I am talking about the technically oriented ones, the ones with a thin layer of mechanical-pencil dust on your clothing—in a word, the geeks—may even want to plug your computer directly into the wall, thus allowing electricity to flow through it. In this case, you'll also need to purchase a "program," or "software," which comes on a "floppy disk," an object the size of a 45 RPM record such as "Shake, Rattle and Roll," which we used to dance to at "record hops" back when Dwight "Ike" Eisenhower was president.

Fortunately for you and the entire fitness movement in general, I have developed a special piece of fitness-oriented software called the "Dave Barry Total Diskette Workout Program." The way it works is, you

THE GEEK

put it in the computer, which asks you to type in your name. Then you type in your name, and the computer forgets it immediately because the truth is that the computer really doesn't give a damn what your name is. It was just trying to be polite.

Next, the computer holds an Interactive Fitness Dialogue with you, wherein it elicits certain facts from you regarding your specific fitness situation, then it evaluates the facts and reports its findings, as follows:

COMPUTER: ENTER THE LAST TIME YOU ENGAGED IN A WORKOUT.
YOU: (Enter the last time you engaged in a workout, such as "just before Thanksgiving" or "World War II.")

COMPUTER   (thinks for a minute, and proceeds): SOUNDS TO ME LIKE YOU'VE DONE ALL THE WORKING OUT YOU NEED TO DO FOR THE FORSEEABLE FUTURE. ALL WORKING OUT MAKES JACK A DULL BOY! HA HA! PLEASE ENTER A LIST OF THE FOODS YOU WOULD LIKE TO EAT TODAY.
YOU: (Enter a list consisting of no more than 100 foods which you would like to eat on that particular day.)
COMPUTER: I DON'T SEE ANY PROBLEM WITH THE FOODS YOU HAVE LISTED. HAVE A NICE DAY.

That's all there is to it! In less than five minutes, you have accomplished, using a computer, a data-processing feat that would take 60,000 trained mathematicians 1.3 billion years to accomplish, and even longer if you let them go to the bathroom! And you will be pleased to learn that this program will also do your income taxes ("YES! YOU CAN DEDUCT THAT! I'M SURE OF IT!").

Choosing the Right Place to Get Fit

Basically you have two options: your living room, or a fitness club. The advantage of getting fit in your living room is that it's free

THE FITNESS CLUB

and you can scratch yourself openly. The disadvantage is that your living room is where you keep your little dish of M&Ms for guests, which means you'll actually gain roughly a pound of ugly fat for each week of your home fitness program.

So you should probably join a fitness club such as you see advertised in the newspapers by photographs of attractive models wearing leotards fashioned from a maximum of eight leotard molecules. Before you join such a club, you should take a tour conducted by one of the fit and muscular staff persons. This person will show you the various rooms and pieces of equipment, then hold your head under the whirlpool until you agree to buy a membership.

Here's a useful checklist of the features a good fitness club should have:

A powerful odor of disinfectant

Various species of hairs in the sinks

Signs all over the place reminding you that the management is not responsible

A loudspeaker system playing soothing musical numbers as performed
by the Dentist's Office Singers

A door that says "WEIGHT ROOM"
that you never venture through because large sweating men go in there
and emit noises like oxen with severe
intestinal disorders

Two women in the sauna who are always there, no matter what hour of
the day or night, talking loudly
about growths in their pelvic regions

Saunas

The word "sauna" is Finnish for "very hot
little room with strangers in it breathing
funny," and people who've tried it agree
that it's a very invigorating experience, provided you get out in time. If the door sticks
or anything, you have about as much chance
of survival as the unfortunate corals who
happened to be residing on that reef where
we detonated the original hydrogen bomb,
because the usual temperature inside a
sauna is 180 degrees, which you may recognize as the recommended final temperature
for cooked turkeys, very few of which live to
tell about it.

This high temperature is, of course, very
good for you because your body contains
traces of toxic minerals such as lead, which
get in there when you get drunk and eat
paint, and the heat helps you sweat them
out. Really, I'm not making this up. Here's a
direct quote from *Shape* magazine, an
authoritative journal:

"Sweating is now a significant route for
eliminating trace elements from the body."

So that's the good news. The bad news, of
course, is that these trace elements have to
go somewhere, presumably onto the sauna
seat, which means if you use a spa sauna,
you're lounging around on a lot of other
people's trace elements.

So what I recommend is that you build
your own sauna at home, which is a lot easier
than you might think. All you need is a few
simple hand tools. (No! I'm *not* going to tell
you which ones! I'm *sick* of making all the
decisions!)

Using your hand tools, construct a hand-
crafted little wooden room that has a bench
inside it and a sign on the door that says
"WARNING! REMOVE ALL CLOTHING
AND JEWELRY AND DENTAL FILL-
INGS AND PACEMAKERS!" Now all you
need is a way to raise the internal temperature to 180 degrees. You could always set
fire to the sauna, of course, but then you'd
have to handcraft a new one every time you
wanted to use it, which would leave you with

A FEW FRIENDS, A FEW BEERS, A HOT SAUNA, AND THOU...

very little time in which to eliminate your elements. So I suggest that you take the more practical route, which is to plug in 40 toasters set to "medium brown." They'll give you all the heat you need, plus you'll get a healthy aerobic workout clambering around in there trying to keep all the little levers pushed down. Keep the number of the Burn Unit handy.

Okay! Now you've bought your fitness outfits, you've found a place to do your workout, and you've built your own sauna. The only remaining question is . . .

When to Actually Start Your Fitness Program

Not today, certainly. You've done enough today! I would rule tomorrow out, also, seeing as how it comes so soon after today. You rush into these things, and the next thing you known you've strained a ligament or something. So I would say the best time to begin would be first thing after Easter, although not the one coming up.

Chapter 3

Women's Total Complete Aerobic Fitness Workout

Warming Up

To understand the importance of warming up, let's take a look inside a typical human muscle:

As we can see, it's very dark inside a typical human muscle. This means that most of the time the individual muscle cells are fast asleep. The purpose of your warm-up routine is to allow these cells to wake up gradually—to stretch, to scratch, to go to the bathroom, etc. If you just start jerking them around, they're going to be very cranky, and they may develop a condition that professional medical doctors call a "Charley horse," which is usually fatal.

WARM-UP NUMBER ONE: CLEARING YOUR MIND OF WORRISOME THOUGHTS

You can't loosen up effectively if you're worried about nuclear war, or the likelihood that somebody might steal your wallet while you're doing your exercise routine. So your initial warm-up step should be to lie down on your back with your knees bent and your feet planted 17 inches apart, then, with your left hand overlapping your right, clasp your wallet to your chest, raise your head to an angle of about 36 degrees Fahrenheit, and watch "Happy Days" or a similar television situation comedy rerun where they never talk about the likelihood of nuclear war, as shown in Figure 1. Hold this position until

FIGURE 1

about a minute and a half before your neck develops a "crick," which is usually fatal.

WARM-UP NUMBER TWO: LETTING YOUR MUSCLES KNOW YOU'RE ABOUT TO START MOVING

Lie facedown on your wallet with your legs together and your arms away from your body at an angle of about 7 degrees, then have a friend or hired servant place his or her face about an inch from your various major muscle groupings, as shown in Figure 2, and say, in a pleasant, musical voice, "Everybody up! Time to start warming up for a Fitness Workout!" Then have your friend listen closely to your muscle groupings for the sound of good-natured cellular grumbling. If necessary, he or she should prod them very gently with the eraser of a number 2 pencil, such as you used on your college boards.

FIGURE 2

WARM-UP NUMBER THREE: PUTTING A TAPE OF LOUD ROCK 'N' ROLL–TYPE WORK-OUT MUSIC ON A GHETTO BLASTER–TYPE STEREOPHONIC LISTENING DEVICE

One thing you have probably wondered about for many years is why musicians who sing rock 'n' roll tend to be extremely thin, if not actually dead, whereas those who sing, say, opera, tend to be humongous wads of cellulite. The reason for this phenomenon, scientists now believe, is that fat cells are actually destroyed by stupid lyrics. In one recent experiment, scientists at the University of Iowa reduced a live 450-pound hog to an object the size of a harmonica in less than six hours by repeatedly playing the chorus to "Shake Your Groove Thing" at it. Other songs with proven fat-reduction lyrics that you'll want to have on your workout tape are:

"My Baby Does the Hanky Panky"

"Yummy Yummy Yummy I've Got Love in My Tummy"

The verse of "We Wish You a Merry Christmas" that refers to "figgy pudding"

Everything Barry Manilow ever wrote

"Ballad of the Green Berets"
"Da Doo Ron Ron"
"My Way"

To put your tape on your ghetto blaster, lie on your back with your legs about 7¾ inches apart and your wallet clamped in your left armpit, raise your right arm gradually until you can insert the workout tape into the ghetto blaster device, press the "play" button, as shown in Figure 3, then gradually return your arm to the floor and just lie there for a while, spent.

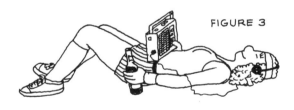

FIGURE 3

The Actual Workout

All warmed up? Great! Let's start getting fit! Do each of the exercises below twice on the first day, 4 times the second day, 8 times the third day, and so on, each day doubling the previous day's number until, after just two weeks, you're doing each exercise over

1,000 times! And hemorrhaging internally! So let's get started!

EXERCISE NUMBER ONE: LEG HEFT

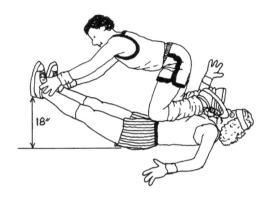

18″

Lie on your back, legs slightly spread, arms resting on the floor, palms down. Have an accomplice grasp you by your ankles and lift your legs about 18 inches then attempt to guess their combined weight.

EXERCISE NUMBER TWO: THIGH GRASP

Lie on your stomach with your face resting on a *New York Times* "Fall Fashion Supplement" opened to a photograph of a model who consumes fewer calories in an entire year than you do at a single wedding

reception. Slowly reach your hands down and grasp yourself by the left thigh, then the right, and then close your eyes and moan quietly in despair for a count of about eight seconds.

EXERCISE NUMBER THREE: SINCERE ANNOUNCEMENT OF INTENTION TO CHANGE DIETARY HABITS

You and a partner stand facing each other about three feet apart, legs comfortably spread, knees slightly bent, eating from individual one-pound bags of Wise brand potato chips. You say, "First thing tomorrow I swear to God I am definitely going to go on a diet, I really mean it." Your partner

responds, "Yes, me too. I definitely will go on a diet also. I believe there is a vat of Lipton brand California-style onion dip in the refrigerator." Then you exchange places and repeat the exercise.

EXERCISE NUMBER FOUR: BREAST DEVELOPMENT

Originally, I was going to use this space to describe an amazing new Scientific Discovery exercise that enables any woman to develop, within minutes, two large, firm breasts such as are regularly featured on television star Loni Anderson. But then I said to myself, "Hey, isn't it time that we, as a liberated society, got over this juvenile and demeaning fixation with breasts?" So I have decided to omit this particular amazing, risk-free, 100 percent effective exercise, although of course if you wish to obtain a copy for the purpose of scientific research, I'd be happy to send it to you just for the asking, plus $29.95 for postage and handling. If you act right now, I'll also send several grainy before-and-after photographs of women who used to look like Olive Oyl but now, thanks to this Amazing Breast Exercise Discovery, cannot walk erect unless preceded by native bearers.

Cooling Down

As we discussed in Chapter 1, when you exercise, your muscle cells take in molecules of oxygen and give off molecules of sweat, which work their way to your armpits. For your cooling-down phase, lie on your back with your arms laced behind your head and your elbows on the floor, thus exposing a maximum of armpit area and allowing the sweat molecules to escape into the atmosphere as harmless BO vapors. This would be an excellent time to start worrying about nuclear war again.

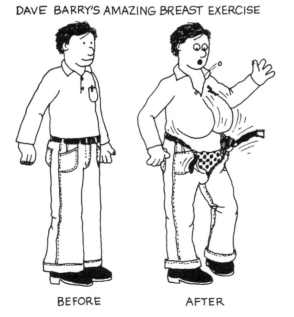

DAVE BARRY'S AMAZING BREAST EXERCISE

BEFORE   AFTER

Chapter 4

Running

An Important Safety Note about Running

In this chapter, I can give you only a cursory overview of running, which is without question the most difficult and complex form of exercise, as is evidenced by the fact that it is the subject of numerous lengthy books costing upward of $14.95. Unfortunately, many members of the general public still labor under the dangerous misconception that running is simply a matter of getting out and running. So before you attempt to do any actual running, I strongly urge you to read a minimum of several books on the subject and to take lessons from a trained running instructor. I also cannot overemphasize the importance of spending large sums of money.

What Kind of Person Should Take Up Running, and What Will Happen to This Person's Knees

Running is the ideal form of exercise for people who sincerely wish to become middle-class urban professionals. Whereas the lower classes don't run except when their kerosene heaters explode, today's upwardly mobile urban professionals feel that running keeps them in the peak form they must be in if they are to handle the responsibilities of their chosen urban professions, which include reading things, signing things, talking on the telephone, and in cases of extreme upward mobility, going to lunch.

That's why at the end of the working day, when the lower classes have passed out facedown in the Cheez Whiz, you can drive down the streets of any middle-class neighborhood in America and see dozens of professionals out running with determined facial grimaces, burning off calories, improving the efficiency of their cardiovascular systems, increasing their muscle flexibility, and ultimately staggering off into the bushes to die. Even as you read these words, thousands of designer-sportswear-clad bodies are rotting in the bushes of suburban America, and the only reason you don't hear more about it is that the next of kin generally don't report the disappearances, because they are quite frankly pleased that they no longer have to listen to the runner blather on and on about his or her cardiovascular development.

Of course, not all runners die in the bushes. Many fail to make it that far, because of knee injuries. To understand why, let's look at this anatomical diagram of the interior of the human knee.

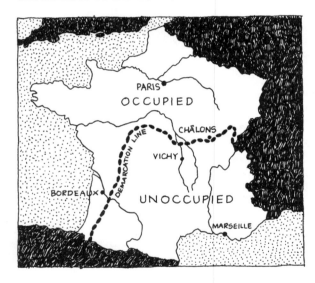

What we can learn from this diagram is that, although from the outside your knee feels like a croquet ball inserted in the middle of your leg, it is in fact a complex organ consisting of bone, muscle, thong, and mucilage, bounded on the west by Spain. The knee provides adequate support for everyday activities, such as renewing maga-zine subscriptions or gesturing at cretins in traffic, but it is not designed to withstand the strain placed on it by running, where each time the runner's foot hits the pave-ment, the knee is subjected to 650,000 kilo-cycles of torque, and even more if the runner has been dropped from a helicopter. This is why it is so very important to choose the right running shoe.

Choosing the Right Running Shoe

Time was, of course, when there were no running shoes, only "sneakers," which were bulky objects that cost $12 and said "U.S. Keds" on the side and had essentially the same size, weight, and styling characteris-tics as snow tires. But today's topflight run-ning shoe is a triumph of sophisticated, computer-designed, laser-augmented, fully integrated, infrared, user-friendly technol-ogy and space-age materials, packed with dozens of medically proven health and safety features, and all combined into a small and lightweight unit that, surprising-ly, costs no more than a black-market infant. Let's take a peek inside a typical running shoe and see how this technological miracle is accomplished.

ABEBE BIKILA MODEL STATIC-BALANCE "ROCKET THUNDERSQUAT" 3000-XT RUNNING SHOE
(INTERIOR VIEW) (SIZE 9-D) (ALSO COMES IN BEIGE)

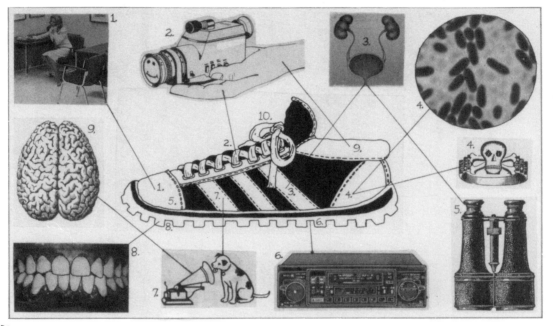

KEY:
1. MAIN STABILIZERS
2. STRESS AVERTERS
3. MAIN DESTABILIZERS
4. AFT MONTAGE SPLINE
5. TORQUE SUBVERTERS
6. ENCROACHMENT VALVES
7. PIGLET'S HOUSE
8. MODEM
9. WENCH INVERTERS
10. STAFF LOUNGE
11. NOT SHOWN
12. NOT SHOWN, EITHER

Choosing the Left Running Shoe

Most running experts and bankers recommend that you wait until you've completely paid for the right running shoe, including insurance, before you plunge in and buy the left. When you do, I urge you to shop around for a shoe that is as similar as possible to the other one, except insofar as which foot it goes on. This is assuming that you intend to wear both shoes simultaneously.

PROPER RUNNING SHOE ALIGNMENT

INTERNATIONAL HAND SIGNALS FOR RUNNERS PASSING EACH OTHER ON THE STREET

| HELLO | MY AORTA HAS RUPTURED | COME BACK, I AM NOT FINISHED |
| I HAVE A KNIFE | I HAVE A SANDWICH | I HAVE JUST VAPORIZED A DOG |

What to Wear
on the Rest of Your Body

You should, of course, wear a specially designed $200 Running Garment made from a synthetic material that has a name like the leader of a hostile reptilian alien invasion force in a space movie, such as "Gore-Tex." The beauty of these materials is that they actually "breathe." Really. At night, if you listen very carefully to your closet, you'll hear your garment in there, breathing and occasionally chuckling softly at some synthetic joke it heard from your dress slacks.

Where to Run

One good place to run is in the Olympic marathon, because (a) you have to do it only once every four years, and (b) you have an armed motorcycle escort, so if people try to thrust liquids and fruits at you, which is a

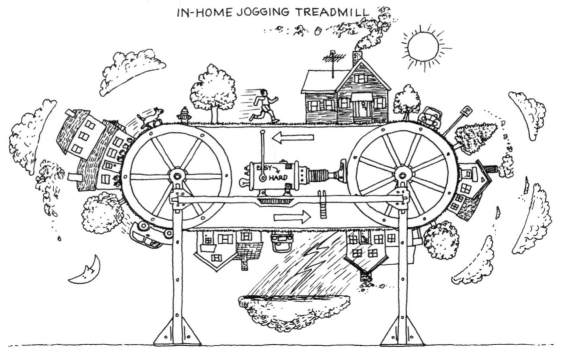

IN-HOME JOGGING TREADMILL

common problem in marathons, you can order your escort to fire a few warning rounds into their chests. The big drawback with running in the marathon, however, is that you have to consort with a bunch of sunken-eyed running wimps, some of whom are not even United States citizens.

This is why many people prefer to run, unescorted, on the streets of their own neighborhoods. The big problem here is dogs, which will view you as an intruder and may attack you, especially if they can smell fear on your body. This is why the wise runner carries a small spray can of a chemical originally designed for use by mail carriers. If a dog attacks, you simply spray this chemical into your nose, and within seconds you don't feel any fear of any damn dog. Be careful that you don't stare directly into the sun.

TO AVOID THIS...

USE THIS...

Chapter 5

Popular Sports

Mankind's need to compete in sports goes back to that fateful prehistoric day, hundreds of thousands of years ago, when a primitive man first picked up a club and a primitive ball fashioned from animal hide, tossed the ball aloft, then whomped the club into the sloping forehead of a primitive umpire. Since then, there has never been a civilization that did not engage in sports. Archeologists digging in what was once ancient Sumeria recently found the remains of a primitive stone jockstrap (see illustration). This goes a long way toward explaining why you see so few Sumerians around.

In ancient Greece, the Olympic games were considered so important that when it was time to hold them, the Greeks would lay down their arms and invite their enemies to do the same. Then the Greeks would snatch up their arms again, whack their enemies into pieces the size of candy corn, and celebrate by having the Olympic games.

Back then, of course, the only events were running naked, jumping naked, throwing things naked, and ice dancing. Today, we have hundreds of sports to choose from. In this chapter we're going to look at some of the more popular modern sports, so you can

ARCHAEOLOGIST FINDS
ANCIENT SUMERIAN STONE JOCKSTRAP

choose the ones you wish to incorporate into your overall fitness program. As I have stressed repeatedly throughout this book, before you embark upon any new form of physical activity, you should notify your doctor's answering service.

Ski Jumping

Ski jumping as a form of exercise has grown immensely in popularity in recent years, especially among people who, because of knee problems, cannot jog. This exciting sport got its start as a symptom of mental illness in northern climes such as Norway and Sweden, where it is cold and dark and there is very little to do except pay taxes. Life is depressing in these countries. Watch any movie by the famous Swedish director Ingmar Bergman, and you'll notice that all that ever happens in the entire two hours is

PORTABLE SKI JUMP SIMULATION DEVICE

depressed people sit around talking Swedish, which sounds like Fats Domino records being played backward, only a little too slow. This is what life in Sweden is actually like, except that it often lasts longer than two hours. After a while, the strain gets to people, and they suddenly leap up, barge out, don skis, and launch themselves off giant chutes.

Americans did very little ski jumping until the television program "Wide World of Sports" began showing a promotional film snippet in which a ski jumper hurtles off the edge of the chute, completely out of control, with various important organs flying out of his body (for a discussion of the various important organs and their functions, see Chapter 1). Fitness buffs saw this and realized that any activity with such great potential for being fatal must be very good for

you, so the sport began to catch on. Today, most major hotels offer ski jumping facilities for the convenience of business travelers. Also, thanks to a new, innovative portable device (see illustration), you can even engage in "simulated" ski jumping indoors! So there's really no excuse not to get into this popular sport, except a will to live.

Peewee Football

Although most people think of Peewee Football as a "kid's game," more and more fitness-oriented urban professionals with a love of physical contact and a sincere desire to lie about their ages have discovered that there's no better way to get rid of frustrations than to lean down, take a handoff (by force, if necessary) from a 48-pound quar-

terback, and plow through an entire team of 8-year-old boys on the way to a 97-yard touchdown run. Not only is it fun, but nutritionists (never mind which ones) tell us that the average 40-year-old male burns off ten extra calories for each child clinging to his ankles!

One word of caution here: If any other urban professionals have discovered your particular Peewee Football league, you want to make sure they play on your team. This is also a good practice to follow with any unusually large eight-year-old boys.

Racquetball

This is a popular sport wherein you and another person go into a white room, close the door, and attempt to injure each other in

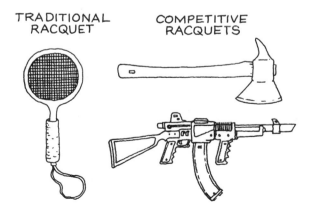

TRADITIONAL
RACQUET

COMPETITIVE
RACQUETS

the eye. Originally, this was done by whacking a ball against a wall in such a way that it would bounce back and strike the other person, but your highly competitive modern player tends to ignore the ball and lunge straight for his opponent. This is why you first should determine the playing style of your potential opponent and then decide whether you need a "traditional" or a "competitive" racquet.

Professional Ice Hockey

Professional ice hockey is an ideal way for the entire family to keep fit. There's something for everyone: the kids will love participating in a loose, freewheeling sport where everybody makes the play-offs and the only activity that is specifically prohibited is selling narcotics to your opponents on the ice; Dad will appreciate the fact that he's improving his cardiovascular efficiency while at the same time fleeing large vicious toothless stick-wielding men whose frontal lobes have been battered into prune-sized masses of scar tissue; and Mom will be pleased to learn that many of the players come from Canada, so she'll have a chance to "brush up" on such French phrases as *Arretez vous! Je suis une femme! C'est ma balle d'oeil!* ("Stop! I am a woman! That is my eyeball!")

Golf

Although golf was originally restricted to wealthy, overweight Protestants, today it's open to anybody who owns hideous clothing. The basic idea is to stand on top of a hummock, squinting into the distance, wager, then saunter over to another hummock, and so on until it's time to drink. That may not sound like much exercise to you, but in fact every one of these activities except drinking consumes calories, as shown by this scientific chart.

Thus we see that in the course of a typical "round" of golf, lasting just four hours, you could burn off enough calories that you could then go out and eat the better part of a slice of Wonder bread with only a minor weight gain.

GOLF ACTIVITY	CALORIES CONSUMED
Ascending hummock	2.04959
Squinting	0.00035
Wagering	0.00102
Descending hummock	1.84958
Sauntering to next hummock	4.02013
Saying things like "You certainly did bogey that par-six eagle nine-iron wedge, Ted! Ha ha!"	0.00076
Tipping wiry youth who carries equipment	0.00007

Swimming

Swimming is one of the best forms of exercise, provided you remember to follow these simple safety rules:

1. NEVER SWIM IN A LAKE OR RIVER. These contain snapping turtles, which have no natural enemies and therefore grow to the size of motel units, plus they tend to be irritable because they mate for life. Lakes also contain giant lake-dwelling carp, which will watch you from the gloomy depths with their buggy eyes, wondering with their tiny carp brains whether you would fit into their mouths.

2. NEVER SWIM IN THE OCEAN. The ocean contains creatures that make the giant lake-dwelling carp look like Bambi.

3. NEVER SWIM IN A SWIMMING POOL. People pee in swimming pools. Oh, I know *you* don't pee in swimming pools, and I certainly don't, but *somebody* does, which promotes the growth of bacteria, which is why swimming pool owners are always dumping in toxic chemicals, to the point where there is virtually no actual water in the pool, just toxic chemicals and dead bacteria and old pee. This is why, as you may have noticed, the actual owner never gets into the pool. He's always off pretending he has to do something important involving the filter.

Pig Lifting

This is probably the quintessential fitness activity for today's upscale young urban professional, who more often than not will forsake the old-fashioned "three-martini lunch" in favor of going to his posh downtown club, sometimes with an important client, for a hard 45 minutes of pig lifting, followed by a soothing hose-down. More than one major business deal has been

forged this way, and the cry "Anyone want to hoist some pork?" is likely to echo down the corridors of power for many years to come.

Fitness for the Business Traveler

Anyone who travels a lot on business will tell you that it isn't easy: eating at a different restaurant every night, having the maid leave little chocolate mints on your pillow, ordering a late-night hors d'oeuvre platter from Room Service while you watch in-room movies such as *Nubile Olympic Gymnasts Visit the Petting Zoo,* and all the other little hassles and inconveniences that go with life "on the road." But for the businessperson who's into physical fitness, there's yet another problem: finding a way to work out. Here are some suggestions.

Without question, the best way to work out in your hotel room is to turn on the television at the crack of dawn and watch one of the morning workout shows featuring the Obscenely Cheerful Leotard Women. Believe me, there's no more invigorating way to start the day than to lie in a darkened hotel room and listen to these women leap around and shout encouragement at you until you work up the energy to hurl your hors d'oeuvre tray at the TV screen and

order Room Service to send up several orders of pancakes immediately.

Center-City Jogging

Although a few forward-looking hotels now offer a service whereby a staff person from a third-world nation will do your running for you while you are in meetings, in most cases you must still attend to this tiresome chore yourself. This isn't so bad if your hotel is located in, say, Nebraska, where the only danger you face on the street is that you might trip over a pig. But it can be a real problem if you're in a large urban area such as New York City, where the vast majority of the people on the street are drug addicts, pickpockets, muggers, rapists, murderers, or partners in advertising agencies.

This doesn't mean you can't run: it means you must take steps to protect yourself. A gun will do you no good. It would just be stolen. No, what you need is a safety device I designed especially to solve this problem—the Urban Runner's Simulated Gaping Chest Wound, which operates on the proven scientific principle that no urban resident will go anywhere *near* a person who is clearly in desperate need of help.

With your Simulated Gaping Chest Wound strapped on, you can jog anywhere you want in New York City, and you'll

attract no more attention than the apparently deceased persons sprawled on the sidewalks, or the random street lunatics holding lengthy debates with individual oxygen atoms. For extra privacy, you can purchase the optional 3,500 Simulated Maggots Eating Your Body accessory.

These devices, incidentally, are part of an entire Dave Barry line of Traveling Executive Fitness Products, which also includes the Heavy Briefcase. This appears from the outside to be a normal leather briefcase, but hidden inside is a 350-pound weight! (There's also a roomy compartment capable of holding your cigarette, or part of your pen.) Executives who regularly carry the

Heavy Briefcase report a dramatic improvement in arm length.

The In-Flight Workout Device is a portable device that, when folded up, fits inside a handy steamer trunk that can be carried on board a commercial aircraft, provided you purchase two adjacent first-class seats for it, yet unfolds after takeoff to form a complete "airborne gymnasium." It features a sophisticated electronic digital computer "brain" that not only monitors your pulse rate, but also has a new and improved electronic circuitry design which we sincerely believe and hope will correct the unfortunate problem whereby it was somehow seizing control of the automatic pilot and steering planes into various mountains, which is, of course, a violation of federal regulations.

Chapter 6

Bodybuilding

Most of us males, at one time or another, have felt like Joe, the scrawny little wimp in the old Charles Atlas advertisement who was humiliated in front of his girlfriend on the beach when the muscular bully kicked sand in his face. As you'll recall, Joe sent away for the Charles Atlas bodybuilding course, then came back to the beach with large, bulging, rippling muscles. When the bully returned, he was extremely impressed and suggested that Joe should also apply oil to his body so that it would have a satiny gleam, and perhaps shave his armpits. Before long, they were very close friends and often helped each other select posing outfits.

BEFORE

AFTER

You may feel that this is the kind of story that "only happens in comic books," but in fact it can happen to you, too—provided you have the discipline, drive, endurance, and just plain old-fashioned guts required to procure the necessary steroids.

Ha ha! Just a little fitness humor there. You don't need to ingest pharmaceutical substances to develop a major body; you simply have to follow the simple-to-follow instructions in this chapter. But first, let's answer some commonly asked questions about bodybuilding.

Q. I'm a man. How large should I let my muscles get?

A. This depends on the size of your head. See, your body has only a certain number (21,796,349,582) of cells. Each of these cells can be either part of your body or part of your head. This means if you make your body bigger, your head has to get smaller, as shown here in these actual unretouched photographs. So you should cease your muscle development as soon as you start noticing the warning signs of severe head reduction, such as:

ACTUAL UNRETOUCHED PHOTOGRAPH SHOWING HOW HEAD CELLS TURN INTO BODY CELLS

Buying lawn ornaments

Having trouble following the plot on "Dukes of Hazzard"

Answering to the name "Vinnie"

If you already meet any of these criteria, you probably shouldn't do any bodybuilding at all. Of course, if you already meet any of these criteria, you're probably still trying to figure out how to get this book open.

Q. Can a woman such as myself engage in bodybuilding?

A. Of course! Although experts have discovered that a woman can never achieve the large muscle mass and definition of a Mister Universe, she can still, with patience, dedication, and hard work, make herself look like this.

Or she can simply have large, realistic depictions of centipedes tattooed on her face.

Q. Once I become huge and muscular, will I still be able to operate a telephone?

A. Push-button, or rotary dial?

Q. Push-button.

A. Probably.

Now that we've answered your commonly asked questions, let's take stock of your current body. Take off all your clothes and stand in front of a mirror, and let's make an objective, professional, scientific assessment. Go ahead! Don't be shy! We can't help you if we can't see what we're working with!

(PAUSE)

So! That's your body, eh?Hahahahahahaha hahahahahahahahahahahahahahahahahaha

hahahahaha! Excuse me. I'm not (choke, gasp) laughing at you, really. I just, ummmmm, I just thought of something funny somebody said to me in 1967. Anyway, looking at your body, I would hahaha hahahahahahahahahahahahahahahaha hahahahahaha! Excuse me. I would say that you hahahahahahahahahahahaha! Whew! Put your clothes back on, okay?

Using this scientific assessment of your current bodily needs as a guide, let's look at the various kinds of bodybuilding equipment.

Weights: A Stupid Idea

Forget about weights. For one thing, they're very heavy, and for another thing, they wreck your body. Look at what they do to your big-time weight lifters, who have turned into 400-pound hairy sweaty shapeless grunting masses of tissue. And the men are even worse. No, you want to take the new, high-tech, scientific route to a better body, with Nautilus equipment.

How Nautilus Equipment Works

Originally designed as a way to keep professional football players from having sex before a game, Nautilus equipment has become an extremely popular bodybuilding aid that not only is costly but also takes up a lot of room. This is because it's actually a series of machines, each specifically designed to develop one of the major muscle groupings (the abductors, the transponders, the trapezoids, the isobars, the quatrains, the bivalves, the Social Democrats, and the gerunds). The idea is that you work a grouping until it can no longer respond to signals from your brain, then you move on to the next machine, and so on until you've worked all your muscle groupings, at which time you signal the attendant, by blinking in a prearranged code, that you wish to be bathed.

I can't go into great detail here about how the various Nautilus machines work, because it would soon become obvious that I don't know. On the next page, however, is a diagram illustrating the operation of a typical Nautilus unit, this one designed to develop facial muscles.

The Trouble with Nautilus Equipment

The trouble with Nautilus equipment is that to use it, you have to join either a spa or a professional football team, which means you're going to spend a lot of time enveloped

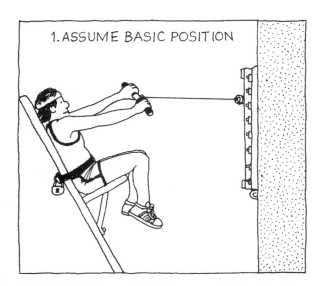

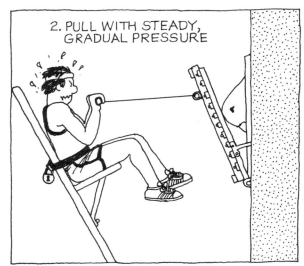

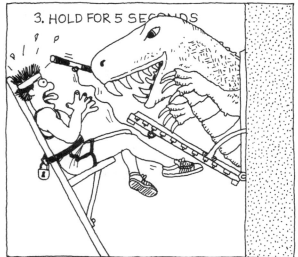

in other people's bodily aromas. So what would be ideal, if only such a thing were possible, would be if somebody would develop a totally new amazing scientific affordable bodybuilding device that you could use in your own home.

Announcing a Totally New Amazing Scientific Affordable Bodybuilding Device That You Can Use in Your Own Home

I am very pleased to be able to announce at this time a major breakthrough in the field of home body devices: the Dave Barry Total Person Workout Device. I'd tell you how good it is, but I'd be violating numerous federal statutes, plus I think you'll be even more convinced by these actual testimonials from imaginary satisfied customers:

"Your Total Person Workout Device has completely changed my life! For example, I can no longer discern colors!"

A.B., Detroit, Michigan

"I was being constantly hassled by vicious youths in my urban neighborhood. I sent away for your device, and within a week they had stolen it!"

C.D., Toledo, Ohio

"What have you done with my wife!"

L.M.N.O.P., Eau Claire, Wisconsin

What's the cause of all this excitement? It's a device that actually costs less than a new home yet yields results like those shown here.

BEFORE

AFTER

Let's turn the page and see this amazing new product!

Both models come in an attractive designer cardboard box telling you which end is supposed to be up and whether or not you should drop it (no). The price is just $799 for the Basic Model and $1,099 for the Really Nice Model, the main difference being that we check the Really Nice Model for vermin. Of course, if you are in any way the least bit dissatisfied with your Device, you simply have to write an angry letter to the employees at your state Bureau of Helping the Consumer, who probably won't be there because they get just about every other day off for cretin holidays like Arbor Day.

FOUR BODYBUILDING EXERCISES USING THE DAVE BARRY TOTAL-PERSON WORKOUT DEVICE

SQUAT   LEAN   TOSS   PUSH-UP

Chapter 7

Nutrition

Why You Should Watch What You Eat

In your great-great-grandfather's day, nobody had to worry about proper nutrition, because people lived on farms and ate wholesome, natural foods. Whenever they needed meat, they just went out and whacked off a sector of the family cow. When they needed bread, they just cut down some wheat, then they threshed it, then they took the grain and starting grinding it up, then they said, "Nah, the hell with it; let's just eat sector of cow tonight."

Today, unfortunately, most cows are grown by giant multinational corporations, who feed them harmful preservatives day and night for the express purpose of killing innocent consumers. Many cows are so full of toxic chemicals that they explode right in the pasture, leaving behind only billowing clouds of greenish fumes, which cause acid rain. You have the same kind of problems with white bread and refined sugar, both of which, if eaten, cause death within hours. This is why it's so important in today's world that you watch what you eat, at least until you get it inside your mouth. After that, it gets pretty disgusting.

How Your Digestive System Works

Your digestive system's job is to turn food into useful body parts. To save itself a lot of aggravation, your digestive system has a

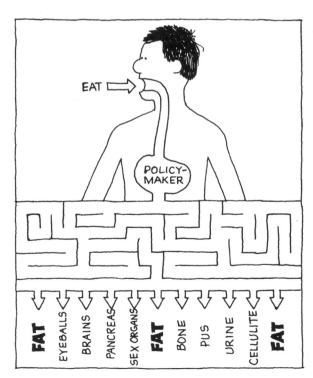

policy whereby it turns a given food into the body part most similar to it. Thus hard-boiled eggs become eyeballs, cauliflower becomes brains, mixed vegetables become the pancreas, Polish sausages become male sexual organs, candy canes become bone, little yellow-covered marshmallow Easter chickens become pus, beer becomes urine, and so on. If you eat a kind of food that does not resemble any known body part, such as a pink Good 'n' Plenty, your body turns it into fat.

Eating a "Balanced Diet"

To make sure your digestive system gets the "raw materials" it needs, at every meal you should eat at least 1 food from each of the 15 Basic Food Families: Fruits, Vegetables, Meats, Fishes, Loaves, Hors d'Oeuvres, Canned Goods, Jellies, Snacks, Shakes, Additives, Eels, Those Little Wax Bottles Filled with Colorful Sugar Water, Pez, and Spam.

What You Can Learn from Reading the Labels on Foods

Virtually nothing. I mean, if the product contains some dangerous chemical, you don't think the label writer, who has a mortgage and kids with braces just the same as you do, is going to risk his job by saying so, do you? Of course not. This is why all labels are written in label jargon, such as "This product contains not less than 0.02 percent of rehydroxylated glutonium or abstract of debentured soybean genitalia, whichever comes first." The more of this kind of jargon you see, the more likely it is that the label writer has something to hide.

So what I recommend is, instead of trying to understand the words on the label, you simply figure out the average number of syllables per word. If the average is two or below, the product is probably safe to eat in small quantities. If the average is three or four, you're probably dealing with a product that causes grave concern in laboratory rats. If the average is five or more, you should set the container down very carefully and flee the vicinity on foot.

About Vitamins

Vitamins are little pills named A, B, C, D, E, and K that the government recommends you have certain amounts of. These recommendations are based on the requirements of the Minimum Daily Adult, a truly pathetic individual that the government keeps in this special facility in Washington, D.C., where he is fed things with names like "riboflavin."

Physicians generally pooh-pooh the value of vitamins, but this is because you can get vitamins into your body without the aid of physicians. If the only way it could be done was for a team of eight surgeons to implant a special $263,000 trapdoor in your head, physicians would say vitamins were the best thing since luxury German automobiles.

The truth is that vitamins are very good for you, and each morning you should take a vitamin A pill, followed by a vitamin D, followed by an E, until you have spelled the healthful mnemonic phrase "A DEAD CAD BAKED A BAD CAKE, ACE." This will probably be plenty of vitamins for you, but be alert for the Four Major Warning Signs of Vitamin Deficiency, which are:

Nosebleeds

A sudden fondness for
Wayne Newton

Unusually thick coats on woolly caterpillars

Death

If you notice any of these signs, you should add the phrase "A BEAKED DAD BEDDED A BEAD-BEDECKED BABE."

Vitamins in Food

Foods contain vitamins. Your mother told you this. She also told you that the vitamins are always in the most repulsive part of the food. If you were eating a potato, for example, she'd say, "Be sure to eat the skin, that's where the vitamins are." They learn this in Mother School. So with any given food, you should always eat the skin or, if it doesn't have a skin, the rind, the core, or the pit. If it doesn't have any of *these,* you should eat the wrapper.

Minerals in Food

Foods also contain minerals such as zinc, iron, magnesium, steel, and aluminum. At least, that's what I'm supposed to tell you. I personally think the whole idea that there is metal in food, especially blatantly soft food such as Twinkies, is absurd. The only idea more absurd is the deranged notion that eating metal is somehow good for you. If God had wanted us to eat metal, He would have given us much better teeth. Thank you.

What about Fiber?

Fiber is definitely the number one hot trend in the world of natural health, threatening to break all the old records set by "pH balance." Remember, back in the 70s, when every product you bought—food, shampoo, tires—was advertised as being pH balanced, even though nobody ever knew what the hell it meant? Well, it's like that with fiber today, and so naturally I recommend you eat all the fiber-rich foods you can shove down your throat. These would be mainly your cotton candy and your Slim Jims.

A Thoughtful Philosophical Discussion of Vegetarianism

This is a touchy subject for me to discuss without having the vaguest idea of what I'm talking about, but here goes. Many people feel it is wrong to eat animals, on the grounds that animals have souls. I would

have to say, although I certainly have nothing but the deepest respect for this position, that this is pretty stupid. I mean, I don't want to offend any religious group, especially if it is armed, but I frankly don't see how anyone can say that *all* animals have souls. Obviously, some animals do: Lassie clearly did, and probably so did Trigger. If anybody ever tries to eat Lassie, I'll be the first one to attempt a citizen's arrest.

But nobody's going to look me square in the eye and claim that, for example, toads have souls. I am not saying that it's okay to eat toads, of course, unless the alternative is starvation, or what they serve you under the

VEGETARIANS ARE EASY TO SPOT AT ROADSIDE REST STOPS

WHERE DOES HAMBURGER COME FROM ?

A. COWS, BULLS, STEERS?   B. PIGS, DOGS, CATS?   C. SHARKS, WHALES, RATS?

heading of "snack" on commercial airliners. I'm just saying we have to draw the line somewhere.

I, personally, follow what I call a "modified vegetarianism" system, under which it is okay to eat meat provided that it has been disguised so you can't tell what kind of creature it came from. A perfect example is hamburger. There is no way to tell, just by looking at a hamburger, where it originated. We believe it is from cows, because we are told this by burly cleaver-wielding men in Chicago with bloodstained garments, but we would not have come to this conclusion independently. So under my system, hamburger is fine.

Lobster, on the other hand, is out. There is no way you could *not* know you were eating a lobster. When you walk into a restaurant, often the first thing you see is a large tank containing lobsters wearing handcuffs and trying to scuttle behind each other so you won't pick them. If you order a lobster, you don't get to use the kind of euphemisms you use with cows, such as "beef" or "steak": you say, "I'll have a lobster," and when they bring it to you, you just get this naked *lobster,* and you're supposed to *eat* it. I think this is wrong, and I imagine it goes without saying that I also feel very strongly about blatant organs, such as tongue.

Chapter 8

Dieting and Weight Control

Do You Weigh the Proper Amount?

To answer that question, locate yourself on the medical chart provided here. Chances are the chart shows that you're above your proper weight. The reason is that you eat too many foods that are high in "calories," which are little units that measure how good a particular food tastes. Fudge, for example, has a great many calories, whereas celery, which is not really a food at all but a member of the plywood family, provided by Mother Nature so that mankind would have

AGE	FEMALE			MALE		
	SMALL	AVERAGE	BIG	SMALL	AVERAGE	BIG
18–25	E	F	A	B	C	D
26–31	F	A	B	C	D	E
32–39	A	B	C	D	E	F
40–50	B	C	D	E	F	A
Over 50	C	D	E	F	A	B
Dead	D	E	F	A	B	C

A—You could definitely stand to lose weight.
B—No question about it, you have a weight problem.
C—Based on your weight, you should get on a diet.
D—It would certainly not hurt you to lose some weight.
E—You are carrying too much weight for your body type.
F—You must make more of an effort to control your weight.

a way to get onion dip into his mouth at parties, has none.

The Simple, Basic, Obvious Truth about Losing Weight

Obviously, the only sane way to lose weight, and to keep it off, is to . . . *Hey!* Who *are* you guys?!! Wait a minute!! You can't just barge in here and . . .

IMPORTANT ANNOUNCEMENT

LADIES AND GENTLEMEN: PLEASE DO NOT BE ALARMED. THIS BOOK HAS BEEN TEMPORARILY TAKEN OVER BY THE INTERNATIONAL BROTHERHOOD OF DIET BOOK AUTHORS. IT HAS COME TO OUR ATTENTION THAT MR. BARRY WAS ABOUT TO TELL YOU THAT—HA HA, THIS IS A GOOD ONE—MR. BARRY WAS ABOUT TO TELL YOU THAT THE ONLY SANE WAY TO LOSE WEIGHT IS SIMPLY TO EAT LESS AND GET SOME EXERCISE. HA HA, WHAT A CRAZY IDEA. OF COURSE, IF IT WERE THAT SIMPLE, THERE WOULD BE NO NEED FOR US TO WRITE ROUGHLY 6,000 LENGTHY NEW DIET BOOKS EVERY YEAR, WOULD THERE? PLEASE ACCEPT OUR APOLOGIES FOR ANY INCONVENIENCE THIS INTERRUPTION HAS CAUSED. WE WILL RETURN MR. BARRY TO YOU JUST AS SOON AS OUR ENFORCEMENT DIVISION, HEADED BY THE PARAMECIUM BROTHERS, ANTHONY AND VICTOR, FINISHES EXPLAINING OUR POSITION IN THIS MATTER TO MR. BARRY THROUGH A PIECE OF INDUSTRIAL DRAINPIPE INSERTED INTO HIS EAR. THANK YOU.

So as I was saying, the only sane way to lose weight is to get yourself on, and then stick to, a regular, planned, conscientious program of purchasing newly published diet books. Here are some that I especially recommend:

The Handsome Sincere Random Doctor Medical Diet

Poop Yourself Thin

The Elvis Presley Memorial Diet

The Total Tapeworm Diet

How to Lose Weight in the Coming Depression

Shed Unwanted Ounces the Orson Welles Way

The Dead Preppy Cat Microcomputer Diet Book

The All-Goat-Products Diet

The Frequent Casual Motel Sex Diet

The Amazing Mother Theresa Weight Loss Plan

All of these books are very excellent, and there are thousands more that are just as good, many of them offering such proven and time-tested features as consecutively numbered pages.

Perhaps the best diet book is *Dessert Makes You Fat*, by Ernst Viewfinder, who

DR. VIEWFINDER EXPLAINING HIS THEORY TO MOTEL FOOD ADMINISTRATOR STUDENTS

has several credits toward his Associate's Degree in Motel Food Administration from Southwest Buford County Community College ("Where the Leaders of Tomorrow Are Frowning at Blackboards Today, Visa and MasterCard Accepted"). His theory is that people get fat because they eat too many desserts, so he has developed a diet designed to encourage you to skip the dessert. Here is a typical day's menu:

BREAKFAST
Froot Loops
Eclairs with side orders of bacon
DESSERT: One slice whole wheat toast

LUNCH
Snickers
Fries
Any number of cheeseburgers
DESSERT: Cottage cheese

DINNER
Dixie cup filled with sugar
Melted Turkish taffy soup
Big lumps of chocolate with fudge sauce
DESSERT: That really pathetic lettuce
that looks like lichen, festooned with clearly
visible insect eggs (no dressing)

I personally tried this diet for several weeks, and I found that not only was I able to skip many desserts, but I didn't need to sleep at all, although near the end they tried to make me.

Common Questions Often Asked about Losing Weight

Q. Do I actually have to read my diet books?

A. No. There is no medical evidence that reading leads to weight loss. Simply keep the books in a prominent location in your home, and occasionally press them against your thighs and buttocks.

Q. Is there any kind of operation I can have that will help me lose weight?

A. There are quite a few such operations, but probably the most effective one, with the fewest negative side effects, is to have an airline pet transporter bonded to your skull with fast-drying epoxy cement (see illustration). This encourages you to eat only those foods which will pass through the mesh door, such as fettuccine and licorice.

Q. What about absurd mechanical weight loss devices, such as those motorized belts that were always shown jiggling the massive hips of pasty middle-aged female character actresses in comedy movies and television shows up through the 1950s?

A. These devices are extremely effective. The fat just melts away. Two of those character actresses, in fact, went on to become Bo Derek and Victoria Principal. This is why you never see those machines in health clubs any more: the clubs took them out because their members were leaving at an alarming rate to accept lucrative film contracts. This is a shame, really, because it leaves the weight-conscious person without any kind of guaranteed, surefire, safe, proven weight loss device. If only somebody would make such a device available to the general public!

Announcing the Dave Barry Guaranteed, Surefire, Safe, Proven, Medically Unusual Weight Loss Device for Human Beings Belonging to the General Public

VICTORIA PRINCIPAL (BEFORE)

The concept for this truly revolutionary device, which came to me one evening while I was throwing up on my shoes, is amazingly simple: If you go around with an object that weighs approximately 350 pounds strapped to your body, you can't help but lose weight! Assuming you don't have a serious accident! So I designed this device with You, the Consumer, in mind, such that you can wear it virtually undetected to work, around the home, on the tennis court . . . even to executions, if these are permitted in your state!

THE DAVE BARRY WEIGHT-LOSS DEVICE FITS INTO YOUR ACTIVE LIFE-STYLE

What the Experts Say about the Dave Barry Weight Loss Device

"Yes! Okay! It is very good! People should buy it! Now please, let us go!"

—A team of leading physicians speaking in unison from inside a concrete structure

"The water used in Tokyo, Yokohama, Kawasaki, and other parts of the metropolitan area is supplied by aqueduct systems!"

—*The Encyclopaedia Britannica* Volume 18 (Taylor-Utah)

Chapter 9

Women's Beauty and Grooming

Thus far in this book, we've concentrated on improving your body. But let's face it: having a great body does you no good whatsoever if you have the kind of face where people are always saying you have a Nice Personality, meaning you can cause crops to fail just by looking at them.

So in this chapter, we're going to take a look at some of the things you can do to your face and hair to give yourself that feeling of inner confidence that says, in the words of the song Maria sang in *West Side Story* just before her lover stabbed her brother to death, "I Feel Pretty." You'll see that you don't have to have been born with great genes to look beautiful; there are lots of simple little "beauty secrets" that can turn even a real woofer into an extremely presentable person, although in your case I would not necessarily rule out plastic surgery.

The First Step toward a More Beautiful You

The most important step, of course, is to recognize that whatever you're currently doing is totally wrong. What you need is a New Look, as you know if you read any of the major women's beauty magazines. Month after month, year after year, they publish the same article, which is "Several Dozen New Ways to Put Makeup on Your Face and Style Your Hair in a Lifelong Futile Effort to Look Like the Model on the Cover."

The reason the beauty experts keep coming up with new looks is that the old ones are all repulsive. You look back at your high school yearbook or, heaven help you, your mother's yearbook, and you see the Looks that were popular years ago, and you wonder how the human race managed to reproduce. You wonder why men and women didn't take one look at each other and sprint in opposite directions until they dropped from exhaustion. Someday your children will say the same thing about the way you look today, which is why we here in the beauty industry are always pushing back the frontiers of knowledge, coming up with New Looks, with no real hope of personal financial benefit beyond the sale of beauty products that cost more per ounce than all but the finest narcotics.

Sometimes, out of the goodness of our hearts, we beauty experts make guest appearances on those morning television shows devoted to a wide range of topics that the folks who run television feel are of interest to women, namely these:

Sex problems

Fashion and beauty tips

Problems that involve sex

Tips on beauty and fashion

Various sexually involved problems

Discussions of how you can become more sexually fashionable and beautiful by means of certain tips

Pasta

What the beauty experts generally do on these shows is select a woman from the audience and point out how she has committed several dozen common major beauty blunders due to the fact that she is not a knowledgeable beauty expert. Their technique is to pick somebody who looks perfectly normal—perhaps even attractive—to the unprofessional eye, then harp away at her until the audience begins to marvel that she managed to get past the studio guards without being mistaken for an escaped boar and shot.

Then they take this pathetic woman, and they give her a completely New Look, offer-ing all kinds of professional beauty tips as they go along:

"Now the most unfortunate facial characteristic of Rhonda here," they say, "is that she has a nose you could hang a garment bag on, so we are going to begin by applying about five-eighths of an inch of base coat to the rest of her head in an effort to make it appear larger. We'll top that off with two coats of sealant, then we'll remove all of Rhonda's current eyebrows and start applying the first few coats of skin dye while we try to think up something we can do about her mouth."

And so on, until Rhonda's face is encased in congealed cosmetic substances to the

A NORMAL BEAUTY MAKE-OVER

BEFORE:
BASICALLY REALLY UGLY
ROUNDED FACE

AFTER:
ADDED BROWNS, SHADOWS,
AND SQUARED-OFF FEATURES

point where her own dog wouldn't recognize her. As the studio audience applauds her New Look enthusiastically, Robert Redford walks onstage and asks her to marry him, and they walk off together, living proof of the advantages of knowledgeably applied beauty products, at least until Rhonda's sealant weakens and her base coat starts falling off in slabs the size of French toast.

What You, Personally, Need to Do about Your Appearance

Unfortunately, we are dealing with the print medium here, so I am unable to consult individually with you in regard to your specific beauty needs, except to say that from this particular angle it appears you ought to give a bit more thought to booger removal. However, I can offer these helpful beauty guidelines for you to bear in mind as you try to achieve your New Look:

GUIDELINE 1

YOUR FACE IS MUCH TOO FAT.

It looks like a weather balloon, for God's sake. Try some puce blush on your cheekbones, if you can locate them, and accentuate those little lines coming out of the

BASIC FACIAL TYPES

MUCH TOO FAT   MUCH TOO THIN

sides of your mouth by filling them in lightly with an Accountant's Fine Point Bic pen.

GUIDELINE 2

I CAN'T BELIEVE WHAT HAS BEEN DONE TO YOUR HAIR.

I am assuming that you didn't pay for that cut. I am assuming that a deranged, near-blind, palsied person wielding pruning shears burst into your room in the dead of night and cut your hair after beating you unconscious. The only thing I can suggest until it grows back out is that you join some sort of religious order that has a mandatory head covering. And when it does grow back, you want to decide which of the three common head shapes, shown below, you have and choose a hairstyle that compliments it.

GUIDELINE 3
I WOULD SAY YOUR EYES ARE YOUR BEST FEATURE.

This is assuming I have to pick something. You want to draw attention to your eyes through subtle use of your lipstick, as this

SHAPE #1   SHAPE #2   SHAPE #3

WRONG   WRONG   WRONG

RIGHT   RIGHT   RIGHT

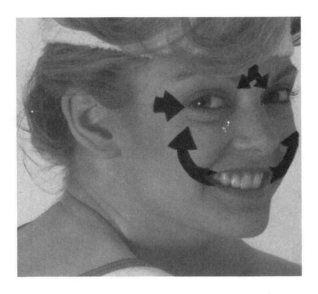

top New York fashion model has done. Note that when I say your eyes are your best feature, I am speaking of them as independent organs. Taken as a set, they are maybe three-quarters of an inch too close together.

Personal Hygiene

After going to all that trouble with your face and hair, the last thing you want to do is go around smelling like a billy goat with a flatulence problem. This is why good personal hygiene habits are so important. Let's review them briefly.

TEETH

You should brush them immediately before having conversations, using a tube of toothpaste with these words printed on the side: "The American Dental Association has found this to be an effective tube of toothpaste when squeezed from the bottom in conjunction with a program of regular payments to a member of the American Dental Association."

GUMS AND ARMPITS

Floss them regularly. If you use the same floss, do your gums first.

HAIR

Shampoo regularly with a shampoo bearing the name of a reputable beauty snot, such as Vidal Sassoon. Also, be alert for dandruff, an incurable disease where little pieces of your head keep falling off until eventually all you have left is two eyeballs on stalks protruding from your neck and you look like a gigantic lobster walking around wearing clothes. Scratching only makes it worse.

FEET

There's an old saying about feet that goes: "I had no shoes, and I pitied myself. Then I met a man who had no feet; so I took his shoes." Better than anything I could think of, this saying illustrates the importance of proper foot care. Each day, you should spend a minimum of an hour examining your feet closely under a 200-watt light bulb and picking at your toenails with various foot care implements available at Woolworth's. This is something the whole family can do together. Stress to your children that they should not mention it to the authorities.

FEMININE HYGIENE

At one time, this important subject would have been considered "too delicate" for a book like this, but all that has changed, thanks to the efforts of the fine people who sell vaginal deodorants via television commercials featuring two Good Friends having a Frank Discussion:

DEBBIE (hesitantly):   Sue, may I ask you something?
SUE: Sure, Debbie. What is it?
DEBBIE: Sue, are you aware that for the past seven years, including at formal affairs such as funerals, you've been emitting an aroma that would fell a buffalo at 90 feet?
SUE (frowning slightly):   Why no, Debbie, I didn't know! Perhaps that is why I have remained a housewife, rather than winning the Nobel Prize for Physics!
DEBBIE: Why not try this?
SUE (examining the label thoughtfully):   Hmmm. New Improved Crotch Bouquet. By golly, I'll try it!
DEBBIE: Not here, for God's sake!

Chapter 10

Men's Beauty and Grooming

As recently as 20 years ago, a man was considered well-groomed if he remembered to remove the little pieces of toilet paper he stuck on his face where he cut himself shaving. But today we live in a liberated era, an era in which men are not afraid to make themselves more attractive by means of beauty aids formerly limited to women—hair coloring, makeup, totally alien plastic substances inserted into the body so as to form bulges, designer dresses, etc.

This is basically a healthy social development. For, as the saying goes, "A man who cares about his personal appearance is a man who is always checking his reflection in store windows." So in this section, men, we're going to suggest some grooming "tips" to help you look more like the lean and cruelly handsome male models in the "Fall Fashion Supplement," and less like the people in your immediate gene pool.

Hair

I will assume that you already shampoo your hair at frequent intervals, that you are not one of those repulsive males who, apparently feeling that there is some sort of grave threat to the world's grease supply, let their hair go for weeks at a time without washing it, such that if one of their pillows ever caught fire, it would burn for days. But men, even if you do use shampoo regularly, it's probably the wrong kind, by which I mean it

GREASER   NEW WAVE MAN

probably consists mainly of shampoo, with perhaps a dash of pH.

This is not good enough. Women discovered years ago that if you want true hair beauty, your shampoo must contain food-stuffs. Some women prefer fruits and vegetables, such as apricot and avocado; others prefer poultry products, such as egg; others prefer liquor, such as beer. Some even prefer—this is the absolute truth coming up here—human placentas, which makes for a *very* expensive shampoo because, believe me, the shampoo factory has to pay the workers a *lot* of money to stuff those suckers into the bottles.

(For a more complete discussion of placentas, see my *Babies and Other Hazards of Sex,* which many experts consider to be, of all the many books available about birth and child rearing, the one that took the least time to write.)

And why is it so important to have food-stuffs in shampoo? I can answer that science question in three syllables: follicles. Follicles are little organs that live in your skull, thousands of them, and produce your hair. To produce hair, they need protein, and to get protein, they need to eat, just as you do. Women are constantly shoving egg and beer down their tiny throats, which is why, as you have no doubt noticed, women generally have gobs of hair. Men, on the other hand,

FOOD

HAIR STALK

SKIN

HAIR FOLLICLES

practically starve them to death—you can eat only so much pH, and then you just don't want to *see* another bite—which is why so many men go bald.

A Sincere Discussion of Baldness

Too often in our insensitive society, baldness is treated as a joke, so let me begin this sincere discussion by stating that, although I am fortunate enough to be blessed with a very full and attractive head of hair, I am very much aware of the anguish and inner torment experienced on a daily basis by you chrome domes out there. I mean, it's not *your* fault you're bald, is it? Well, okay, it *is* your fault because you let your tiny helpless innocent follicles, which had never so much as said a mean word to anybody in their whole lives, suffer a horrible death by starvation while you were out laughing and eating pizza with friends, but there's no point in dwelling on that now. The question is: What can you do about your unfortunate condition?

One approach, of course, is to get a wig. The advantage of wearing a wig is that you don't look quite as stupid as you would if you went around with a giant red clown nose on. The main disadvantage is that a wig costs a lot more than a large, hand-lettered sign around your neck that says "WIG," which is equally effective.

Another approach is to get a hair transplant. This is a procedure whereby a person who has completed all three weeks of Hair Transplant School, which he enrolled in because he flunked Whack-a-Mole-Game-Machine Maintenance School, takes hair from somewhere else on your body and puts it on top of your head. The advantage of this approach is that you do, in fact, end up with

CAN YOU GUESS WHICH MAN IS WEARING AN ACTUAL WIG ? (ANSWER BELOW)

A. TYPICAL ARTIST   B. TYPICAL MINISTER   C. TYPICAL HENCHMAN   D. TYPICAL REPUBLICAN

ANSWER: E

hair growing on your head. The disadvantage, of course, is that it has to come from somewhere else on your body, which means either (a) you have hair growing up there that originated in your armpit or some other locale so disgusting I don't even want to talk about it, or (b) they have to take the hair off the side of your head, which is not necessarily a great stride forward for you in the looks department (see illustration).

HAIR TRANSPLANTS ARE BECOMING COMMON

Finally, there are ads for all kinds of alleged "miracle" hair-growing pills, creams, lotions, and potions in the backs of sleaze-ball publications such as *Penthouse* and *American Beet Farmer*, which make all kinds of outrageous claims such as they can "stop the spread of baldness" and "restore lost hair" and even "grow hair on a billiard ball." These claims, of course, are totally false, except the one about the billiard ball, which government researchers recently discovered is true, the drawback being that many of the balls also developed tumors.

So unfortunately, balding men, there is little to offer you in the way of hope at this time. If only somebody would develop a proven scientific guaranteed effective totally safe miracle hair-growth substance!

(News item)

SCIENTISTS LAUD DAVE BARRY PROVEN SCIENTIFIC GUARANTEED EFFECTIVE TOTALLY SAFE MIRACLE HAIR-GROWTH SUBSTANCE

BUFFALO OR ST. LOUIS—Scientists wearing white smocks here have announced that in proven scientific tests, the

Dave Barry Miracle Hair-Growth Substance did, in fact, bring new life to dead hair follicles belonging to volunteer bald persons who were scientifically monitored as they slept on street grates.

"As this enlarged photograph shows," explained Chief of Research Dr. Ernst Viewfinder, "most of the follicles of the untreated volunteers are small and dead—not unlike, I might add by way of a humorous aside, some of the untreated volunteers themselves, ha ha. But in these photographs of the treated volunteers, we can see that the Dave Barry Miracle Hair-Growth Substance has brought their scalps back to life, with sleek and happy follicles the size of adult mice, in some cases completely crowding out the brain! This could well be what happened to Vidal Sassoon."

Skin

What do women find attractive when they look at a man's skin? Bumps. Yes, bumps. Why do you think women fall all over Robert Redford while virtually ignoring you and me? Go watch Redford in a movie sometime, and you'll see that he has a number of facial bumps, which look during the extreme close-ups to be big enough to play polo on, and which, as far as I can tell, are the only major physical characteristic in which Robert Redford and I differ.

So what I am recommending, men, is that as part of your daily grooming ritual, you apply small globulets of Silly Putty to your face, as shown in the illustration, so as to render yourself irresistible to the opposing sex. I regret to point out, however, that Silly Putty comes in only the Caucasian skin hue,

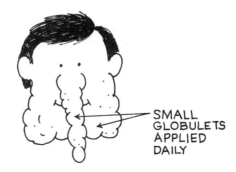

SMALL GLOBULETS APPLIED DAILY

which is blatant discrimination against those members of minority groups who also wish to install facial bumps, and I think those of us who are still liberals ought to sit right down and write hostile letters about this to our Congresspersons.

Makeup

Makeup is definitely the coming thing in male grooming. Oh, I know what you're saying. You're saying, "No *way*. No *way* am I going to put on makeup!" But of course that's exactly what you said about bikini underwear, and hair spray, and blow-dryers, which, if you had used them in a locker room 15 years ago, would have resulted in a situation where if you entered the shower, the other men would have fled from you in very much the way the residents of Tokyo fled from Godzilla, but which are common grooming articles today.

Yes, men, you might as well face it: it won't be long before we're *all* wearing make-up. And the last thing you want to do is get left behind on this trend and end up looking ludicrously out of date, like the unfortunate individuals you occasionally see who still wear white patent leather shoes and matching belts and always look like assistant deputy sewage commissioners from small towns where the highest form of cultural activity is reading the drive-thru menu at Burger King. So what I recommend you do is gradually start introducing makeup into your grooming routine—a little blusher, a little eye liner, a touch of lipstick—and see if you don't start making a big impression at your office, maybe even start attracting the attention of people as high up as vice president, people who once seemed unaware you even existed, but who suddenly start looking at you for 20 and 30 seconds at a time on the elevator and trying to discreetly read your security badge.

Chapter 11

When You Get Sick

Even the healthiest person, if he follows the fitness program described in this book, will eventually need medical care. Fortunately, we Americans live in a nation where the medical-care system is second to none in the world, unless you count maybe 25 or 30 little scuzzball countries like Scotland that we could vaporize in seconds if we felt like it.

What we're going to talk about in this chapter is how you can become more aware of the various problems that your body can develop, so that you'll be better able to worry about them. We'll also talk about how, if you actually do become sick, you can explain your problems to the medical-care establishment in such a way that it does not immediately yank out a useful organ.

How You Can Tell When There Is Something Wrong with You

Trained medical personnel detect illness or other bodily problems by looking for "symptoms," the major ones being these:

  Aches
  Pains

A total absence of aches or pains
Bullet holes
A feeling of not keeping up with inflation
A leg bone sticking out through the skin
Never having the correct change
A stoppage of heart or brain activity
Irritability

Get in the habit of checking yourself every 20 minutes or so for these symptoms. When you notice one, you should immediately follow this emergency procedure:

1. Take two pills containing a Scientifically Proven Painkilling Formula that has been advertised on television by a reliable avuncular spokesperson such as Robert Young.

2. Phone your office to tell them that you won't be in for several days and could somebody please remember to discard any interoffice memoranda aimed at you. If you have no office, you should phone your

mother and have her confirm that there is definitely Something Going Around.

This course of treatment will cure you most of the time. If it doesn't, you probably have a serious illness, which means you should call your physician's answering service and make an appointment to go into his office the following month and sit in the waiting room for an hour and 45 minutes reading *National Geographic*. If *that* doesn't work, you should go to a hospital emergency ward and inflict a gunshot wound on yourself, thus increasing the odds that you will see an actual doctor to nearly 40 percent.

Dealing with Doctors

To get the most out of a doctor, you have to understand how he perceives the world, which is best summed up by the last sentence of the Hippocratic Oath:

"AND ABOVE ALL, REMEMBER THAT THE PATIENT HAS NABISCO BRAND SHREDDED WHEAT FOR BRAINS."

YOU MUST BE PREPARED TO TAKE EXTREME ACTION IN AN EMERGENCY WARD SITUATION

Yes, doctors tend to feel just a tad superior to the general public, but this is understandable. Doctors are generally smart people, the kind who were attending meetings of the National Honor Society while you were leaning out the study hall

SOME GUYS FROM HIGH SCHOOL WERE EASY TO PEG...

DAVID BARRY
Business Education

May 16 –"David"– Band, 9 ; Chorus, 9 ;
Gentlemen Songsters, 9 ; Model Club,
10 ; Future Journalists of America, 10 ;
Likes mashed potatoes, hot dogs,
typewriters, and pet fish. Parents:
Mr. and Mrs. Sylvester Barry.

PRESTON BAINBRIDGE, III
Academic

July 4 –"Little Doc"– Football, 9,10,11,
12 ; Basketball, 9, 10,11,12 ; Golf, 9,
10,11,12 ; National Honor Society, 9,
10,11, 12 ; Future Doctors of America,
9,10,11,12 ; National Medical Merit
Scholarship Recipient; Band, 9,10,11,12;
Gentlemen Songsters, 9,10, 11, 12 ;
Homecoming King ; Varsity Club President, 10, 11, 12 ; Student Council, 9,10,
11,12; Student Council President; Play,
9,10,11,12 ; All-American Golfer, 9,10,
11,12; National Drug Institute Academic
Award, 12; Likes blondes, weejuns,
Corvettes, white clothes, and chasing
ambulances in his red Triumph.
Parents: Dr. and Mrs. P. Bainbridge, II.

window seeing if you could spit on passing nuns. In college and medical school, doctors spend years associating with other smart people and learning complicated things like the location of the pituitary gland. When they get out, the last thing they feel like doing is consorting with a bunch of cretin patients, who not only have no idea where the pituitary gland is, but also are often sick besides.

So the important rule to remember when you're dealing with a doctor is this: *never* tell him what you think the problem is, even if you're absolutely certain. If you tell him what you think, he'll become irritated and go out of his way to prove you're wrong:

YOU: Doctor, I think I have suffered a knife wound to the stomach.
DOCTOR (sneering):   Oh you do, do you? And what makes you think that?
YOU: Well, several hostile urban youths accosted me on the street and stuck a knife in my stomach. See? Here's the knife handle, sticking out of my stomach.
DOCTOR (examining your foot):   That could be caused by any number of conditions, such as an amalgamation of the pyloric valve or an interdiction of the right epistolary oracle. I'm going to send you to the hospital for some tests next week.

The phrase "send you to the hospital for some tests" is medical code for "drain all the blood out of your body." Blood removal is the primary form of health care in the United States, and it has been ever since April 4, 1906, when the founder of the Mayo Clinic, Dr. Ted Clinic, happened to be cutting open diseased woodland creatures, as was his wont, and made an amazing discovery: all of the creatures contained blood. He concluded that blood must be a leading cause of disease, which is why today when you go into the hospital, various personnel are always lunging at you with needles. They are very conscientious about this because they don't want to get a nasty note from the doctor ("3 PM—Patient still contains traces of blood! Let's not let this happen again").

If blood removal doesn't work, they start taking out your organs. Usually they start

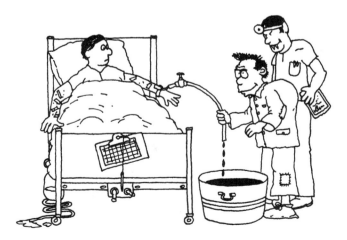

with organs you have two of, such as kidneys, then move up to the really vital ones, so it's very important that you convince the doctor you're getting better while you still have a chance to survive:

DOCTOR: So! How are we feeling today?
YOU (hastily): Fine! Great! Never felt better!
DOCTOR (frowning at your chart): Really? Are you sure? Because I see by your chart here that you still have several organs left, and we could . . .
YOU (staggering out of bed, trailing intravenous tubes): No! No! Look! I feel terrific! (You attempt a deep knee bend, then collapse in agony.)
DOCTOR: Okay, but I'll be back to check on you in an hour.

Paying for Your Hospital Treatment

Always examine your hospital bill closely. It should look like this:

Aspirin tablet $11.05

Little Dixie cup for water to wash aspirin tablet down with 6.80

Water.. 31.80

Removal of childproof cap from aspirin bottle (Dr. Viewfinder)...... 460.00

Removal of little tuft of cotton from aspirin bottle (Dr. Beaner) 385.00

CAT scan from when Dr. Spinnaker thought he might have heard a little whistling noise in the patient's chest that was probably nothing but You Always Want to Be Sure about These Things 87,354.50

Consultation among Dr. Spinnaker, Dr. Viewfinder, Dr. Beaner, Dr. Whelk, Dr. Pilsner, and Dr. Frackmeyer while they were peeing (per doctor)....................................... 275.00

Also Dr. Whelk mentioned it to Dr. Hogworth at the polo match... 340.00

Gratuity....................................... 85.00

If, after examining the bill carefully, you feel satisfied that all the dollar amounts are lined up neatly on the right-hand side, you should submit it to your insurance company, which will, without even looking at it, send it back to you with a testy note telling you that you filled out the forms all wrong. This will give you time to sell your house and children to raise the cash you'll need for when you finally get everything filled out right and the insurance company notifies you that the only thing you're actually covered for is 60 percent of the Dixie cup.

Home Emergency First-Aid Chart to Be Kept Posted on the Bulletin Board underneath the Coupons That, If You Save Up Ten of Them, Get You a Free Medium Pizza

HOME EMERGENCY	TREATMENT
Decapitation.	Elevate head; shriek for assistance.
Victim has swallowed fabric softener.	Induce vomiting by showing the victim a videotape of that speech Richard Nixon gave about his mother after he resigned.
Victim has swallowed a can of chicken gumbo soup.	So? What's so bad about that?
You don't understand. Victim has swallowed the actual *can*.	Oh. Is this by any chance the same victim that swallowed the fabric softener?
Yes, it is.	Boy, that victim has a real problem.
I'll say.	Say, you're kind of cute. What are you doing for dinner?

Chapter 12

Fitness Q and A

Fitness and the Expectant Mother

Q. I am currently pregnant to a considerable degree. Instead of trying to keep fit, may I just lounge around watching "Days of Our Lives" and reading *Glamour* Magazine?

A. No! These are the 80s, for God's sake, and *nobody* is excused from being fit! *Especially* you expectant women! If you just let your body go during pregnancy, after the baby comes, you're going to look as though a team of plastic surgeons have implanted a 35-pound mass of Wonder bread dough under the skin around your hips and thighs. But if you continue to care for your body, if you exercise regularly and maintain your muscle tone, the mass will have a much firmer consistency, like congealed rubber cement.

Of course, a pregnant woman can't do the same exercises as a normal person. Most gynecologists, for example, frown on the pole vault after about the seventh month. But there are still some exercises that work very well for the mother-to-be, such as:

1. TRY TO TOUCH THE WALL. Stand in a relaxed fashion with your arms over your head and your abdominal area forming a large tissue mass directly between you and the wall. Now gradually lean for-

STEP 1

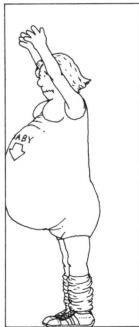
STEP 2

ward until your arms touch the wall, if such a thing is possible, and then return to the full standing position.

2. TRY TO GET OUT OF A CAR. Have several burly friends somehow place you behind the wheel of a 1979 Chevrolet Chevette, or some equally absurd little car, then have them time you as you attempt to get out of it in such a way that your undergarments are not clearly visible from other planets. Eight minutes is the world's record.

3. KNEE CLENCH. Go to a nice restaurant with friends and attempt to get all the way to the appetizers without going to the bathroom more than twice.

Q. What about fitness for the fetus?

A. You should indeed embark upon a rigorous program of fetal fitness, for otherwise the fetus will be born pasty and flabby and lacking in muscle definition, and in later life it may have trouble getting accepted by the better aerobic dancing institutes. Of course, getting the fetus to exercise is not easy, any more than teaching the fetus to read is easy, but if you truly are a Concerned Parent, you will find a way.

I particularly recommend a new product developed by the fine people who make Nautilus equipment. It's called the "Feta-

lus" (see illustration), and it's specially designed for the fetus to use in the womb. It's a very effective device and well worth the cost, although to be perfectly frank the insertion process is not everybody's cup of tea.

Some Helpful Answers for People Who Smoke

Q. I'm a smoker, and . . .

A. You're a what?

Q. I'm a smoker, and I'd really like to . . .

A. You are slime, you know that? You are raw industrial sewage.

Q. Yes, I know. I really want to quit. I just hate . . .

A. Why don't you just suck on the exhaust pipe of a poorly tuned automobile, huh? Why don't you just go around spraying Agent Orange on your fellow restaurant patrons?

Q. Of course you are absolutely right. It's just that it's so hard to stop, and I'm getting desperate, and I was hoping that maybe you'd have some tips on how . . .

A. I'll tell you one thing. If you *ever* try to ignite one of those repulsive toxic objects in a restaurant where I am dining, I shall order a reputable brand of designer carbonated water and forcibly pour it into your nasal passages. Do I make myself clear?

Q. Yes, and I can certainly understand why you feel that way.

A. Well, you'd damned well better.

Q. Thank you.

A. Get out of my sight before I vomit.

Fitness and the Afterlife

Q. I am very, very proud of my body. I have calluses on the top of my head formed by bumping into things because I walk around looking down at my various major muscle groupings. My question is: What will happen to my body when I die? Who will take care of it? Will it become soft and shapeless?

A. You will be pleased to learn that the long-neglected field of postmortem fitness has received a real "shot in the arm" lately with the emergence of the EternaBody chain of fitness centers, each equipped with the patented Cryo-Physique Room, which is very much like a sauna, except that instead of exposing living people to heat, it lowers the temperature of dead people to approximately 325 degrees below zero, at which temperature they acquire a firmness of muscle tone that we normally associate only with world-class bodybuilders and certain minerals.

Fitness and Sex

Q. About a year ago, my husband got on a rigorous fitness program, and he definitely looks much, much better. The problem is, he has taken to viewing our lovemaking as primarily a form of exercise. Like, for example, he wears ankle weights and Heavy Hands, which are no picnic

during foreplay. Also, I have a problem with the idea of having my sexual partner, at a very intimate moment, if you get my drift, shout his pulse rate into a tape recorder. Don't you think he's carrying this too far?

A. Absolutely. First of all, the Heavy Hands aren't doing him nearly as much good as dumbbells would, and second, I see no reason why he can't simply use a felt-tipped marker to jot his pulse rate down quietly on an exposed patch of your skin.

BEFORE

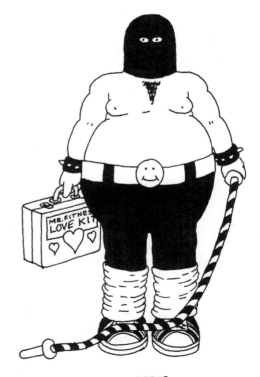

AFTER

Fitness and the Third World

Q. I'm a part of a team of CIA operatives currently operating in a fungal, lice-ridden Central American nation that I, of course, cannot reveal the name of because it's a secret. Our main mission here is to win over the local peasantry to the cause of Freedom and Democracy via a two-pronged program of (a) teaching them how to make sandwiches, and (b) shooting suspected opposition peasants in the head. What I was wondering was, do you think it would help if we also sponsored Dancercise classes?

A. Sounds like a winner! There's nothing that backward peoples enjoy quite so much as dancing, to judge from any number of comical old movies I have seen, wherein the natives are always leaping around and putting Bob Hope in a large iron pot. Be sure your peasants wear an approved style of leg warmer, which the Department of Defense will be able to procure for you at a cost of $63,400 per leg.

Postwar Fitness

Q. What preparations has the government made to insure that our top federal officials will be able to remain fit in the unfortunate event of a total thermonuclear war?

A. At the first sign of trouble, these officials will be whisked to a giant underground Strategic Fitness Facility guarded by vicious federal dogs. This facility will be staffed by a corps of female personnel who have been chosen for their knowledge of postnuclear aerobic routines as well their overall body tauntness. Also there will, of course, be a sauna and several lead-lined racquetball courts, although, as one top government planner put it, "It won't be a picnic in there. Towels will be at a premium."

Office Fitness

Q. **I am employed by a large corporation, and I work in an office where my primary responsibility is to discuss "General Hospital" with Helen and Louise. As you can imagine, this does not involve a great deal of physical activity, and I have, quite frankly, developed a rear end which could serve as a bulldozer-flotation device. So I was wondering if you can suggest any kind of fitness program that a person can do at her desk.**

A. Certainly. Each morning, during a quiet period, quietly slip off your shoes, push your chair away from your desk, and engage in five minutes of gentle stretching, followed by five minutes each of toe touches, dressage, the luge, and the 400-meter butterfly. Of course, some of these activities may require minor changes in your office routine, to allow for such things as feeding

HAVING A DESK JOB OFTEN LEADS TO SLIGHT WEIGHT DISTRIBUTION PROBLEMS

the horse, but I'm sure your employer will have no objection once you threaten to file a gigantic class-action suit alleging you are being discriminated against on the basis of being pear-shaped.

Index